Tried and Tested

My First Fifty Years

Tried and Tested

My First Fifty Years

Maureen Nkandu

Gadsden Publishers

Gadsden Publishers
P.O. Box 32581, Lusaka, Zambia

ISBN 978 9982 24 1045

*In memory of
Mum and Dad*

Introduction

Everybody's life is a story. There are the good parts and the bad parts; the happy and the sad; funny, silly and sometimes even very scary parts. And when we tell a story we never tell it the same way twice. But here's one way to tell my story - the only truthful way. May 1, 2017 was my 50th birthday and I felt the need to write this autobiography now to share the events and experience of my life in the last half century. As I begin the next half of my life, I hope that my story will motivate, inspire, enthuse and encourage many who read this book.

How it all Started

It was a cold winter's day. I was polished and confident. Although I was twelve years old, my mother gave me a bath that morning - a good scrubbing to make sure that I was clean and dressed properly. It was an uncomfortable experience because I always bathed myself, but this day was different. I had an important task ahead.

A few weeks earlier officials from the Zambian government had visited my school - Lusaka Girls Primary School - to request that students enter a national writing competition. We were to write a speech on behalf of all Commonwealth children to be read out to an important global figure.

I was among the three finalists from my school, who had made it to the shortlist of fifteen scholars from schools in the city. The list was narrowed down to three, and then finally, my speech was chosen. I had written about issues I felt important for young children and what the Commonwealth needed to do to address them.

My parents were ecstatic when they heard from my headmistress and foreign affairs officials that my speech was selected. They wondered how at my young age, I could have known or even understood what the Commonwealth was. What they didn't know was that I frequented my father's small library and perused his books almost daily.

I enjoyed reading aloud. I used to pick a book from the shelf and practice reading. Among the books I read frequently was one on the Commonwealth Secretariat and a report on its last Heads of State and Government Summit in London in 1977.

Although I did not fully comprehend the content, I enjoyed reading about issues outside my country. My father was a journalist who travelled around the globe. His reports back to the family on his assignments and adventures excited me. I wanted to learn more. So, I took to reading the books in his study or any other book I found lying around.

I also enjoyed writing and I would write stories to read out to my classmates. They agreed that I was a good speech writer and public speaker, although my insistence on being a TV star one day, brought ridicule and teasing from my colleagues.

It was July, 1979, the year the United Nations declared the International Year of the Child. Zambia hosted the Commonwealth Summit that year.

It was an important time in the history of the country which was at the forefront of the liberation struggle in Southern Africa. I had appealed in my speech to the Commonwealth to do something about the plight of children in Southern Rhodesia (Zimbabwe), South West Africa (Namibia) and South Africa who were affected by the fight for self-rule and the end of apartheid. I learned about their plight from the evening TV news and my father's two-band wireless radio, which he listened to almost religiously every evening after supper.

It was time to go to school. My parents were very nervous. My mother was dressed like a queen. She wore a beautiful pink dress with a matching long jacket. She had white shoes, white gloves, and a white hat and carried the white clutch handbag which my father bought for her in Vietnam and which she only carried to special occasions. My father was just as polished in a black suit, with a white shirt and red tie. He always spoke about how being well dressed gave one confidence. Looking at my parents' sense of dress that morning, I realised that the occasion at which I would be the centre of attention was a very important one. But I was not nervous. In fact, I looked forward to it.

As we drove to Lusaka Girls Primary School, scores of people, mostly children had lined the streets for kilometres to welcome the visiting delegates. Several important-looking people came forth to meet me as I got out of my father's car. They took me to the headmistress, Mrs Chikula's office and went through the drill of the day. They wanted to make sure that I was fine and ready.

My teacher, Miss Old, was a nervous wreck and she kept asking me if I was scared. "No I'm not," I said, wondering why they were all making a big fuss over nothing. I was used to speaking in public, but I had no idea how big this occasion would turn out to be.

Soon I heard sirens and police motorcycles and saw a lot of men in dark suits and sunglasses running all over the place. Hundreds of people including school children had gathered at the school. Students were well dressed and neat. I was taken to the centre of the small staircase where I was to read out my speech. My mother who was standing behind me stepped forward to ensure that my hair ribbon was in place. She was gently pushed back by a white man in dark glasses whom I later found out was a security official from the UK.

Then the vehicles with the important guests arrived. One after the other, the dignitaries stepped out and walked towards me. They came up to the staircase where I was standing and smiled at me. I smiled back, blissfully oblivious of how powerful they all were. Then I got the sign to start and I began reading my speech…

"Your Majesty Queen Elizabeth the Second; Your Royal Highness the Duke of Edinburgh, Prince Phillip; Your Excellency the Prime Minister of Britain, Honourable Margaret Thatcher; The Party Secretary General of UNIP, Mr Mainza Chona; The Secretary General of the Commonwealth, Sir Shridath Ramphal; The Duke of York, Prince Andrew, the Royal Party, international guests and government officials; fellow students; ladies and gentlemen. On behalf of all Commonwealth children………." I went on reading my five minute speech confidently and without a fluff.

When I finished, I curtsied as I was told to do during rehearsals, took a few steps down the small stairway and shook Queen Elizabeth's hand and greeted all the other high level guests who were with her. I handed over my speech to the British Monarch who congratulated me for a strong and well delivered message. The Queen asked me what I wanted to be when I was older and I responded as I always did… "A TV Star." They all laughed and applauded. They loved my confidence. "Well, so you will be," said Queen Elizabeth II.

The royal party then ascended the stairs where they were introduced to my parents. My mother was already in tears. She couldn't believe that she had met and shaken hands with the famous Queen of England and other important people. Her face was red.

I was whisked away by men from the secret service as dozens of photographers ran after me to try to take pictures. After the guests' brief tour of the school, my parents and I were invited to join the visiting delegation for a state luncheon. My father's not-so-new Fiat 128 joined the convoy of flashy expensive cars and we excitedly drove with the rest of the motorcade. This was too much for my mother who could not stop crying. But I was enjoying every moment of it. I was glad that I had read the speech well and had done my school and my family proud.

The following day, I was the hero of the school. All the children wanted to be my friend. I was featured in the newspapers and others had seen me on TV. I always knew that I would be famous one day but I didn't think it would come so soon. At home, my siblings nicknamed me 'the queen'. I truly felt like royalty. I was to remember this experience for the rest of my life.

Twenty years later, as a senior journalist with South African Broadcasting Corporation, I was assigned to cover the 16th Commonwealth Heads of States and Government meeting in Durban. I was among the TV anchors who were interviewing high profile guests and providing commentary and analysis on the Summit.

On the eve of the official opening a few people were invited to a state banquet hosted by the South African Government. Some of my workmates and I were among the invited guests. Before dinner, while having cocktails in the holding room, I narrated to my colleagues the story of how I met the Queen in 1979 and everything that happened on that glorious day exactly twenty years earlier.

As we chatted and enjoyed the early part of the evening, we were informed that Her Majesty was to come into the room to 'meet and greet' before going into the banquet hall. I was very excited. It would be nice to see the Queen again, although I doubted that I would even get the chance to speak to her and remind her of when we met when I was a little girl.

Soon a loud voice announced the entrance of Her Majesty. I and dozens of others had lined up in the room. To my amazement, Queen Elizabeth II walked directly to where I was standing and greeted me. At that point everything in the room seemed hazy – like I was in a trance. I couldn't believe that of all the people in the room the Queen walked straight up to me and greeted me.

The British Monarch asked my name, and what I did. After telling her who I was, I broke the tradition of not speaking to royalty unless you are spoken to, by quickly slipping in that I had met her Majesty twenty years earlier when I read a speech to her. I strongly felt the need to remind her! "Oh yes, at the girls' school in Lusaka. I do remember," said the Queen. "Did you ever become a TV star?" asked Queen Elizabeth. "Yes Your

Majesty, I did. I now work for Television here in South Africa," I answered.

"Oh wonderful, well done," said the Queen, and she moved on to greet others.

I nearly burst into tears of joy. When I was younger, I didn't understand why my mother cried when she was delighted. Now that I was much older, it made sense to me. Happy times evoke emotions.

After dinner people came up to congratulate me for being singled out by royalty. "There must be something special about you. The Queen does not chat with ordinary people that long, but she spent almost thirty seconds with you," they told me.

Well, what we all did not know was that during the cocktail drinks in the waiting room, Buckingham Palace and British undercover officers overheard my story about how I'd met the Queen when I was twelve years old. They in turn informed Her Majesty that there was a lady in the audience whom she had met earlier. They briefed her on what I was wearing and suggested it would be good for her to walk directly up to me when she entered the room and have a very brief chat. Good and well managed public relations! So, it wasn't just a random gesture by Queen Elizabeth II that evening. It was well planned.

Early Childhood

I was born into a well-to-do middle class family. My father, a journalist and politician, was a freedom fighter in the early 1950s and '60s. It was a critical time of transformation for a number of African countries. The strong wind of pan-Africanism espoused by Ghana's founding father Dr Kwame Nkrumah, Ethiopia's Emperor Haile Selassie and other anti-colonial stalwarts, blew across the continent, yielding several independent states.

My mother was a social worker although she spent most of her early adult years as a housewife. She later became a successful business woman and, sadly, a victim of her success.

Zambia gained independence from Britain on 24th October, 1964. I was born three years later on 1st May, 1967. I came from a very big family. My father was married twice before he met my mother. He had six children from his two previous wives - three sons and three daughters. I heard stories from my mother that her husband left his first wife because she drank too much alcohol and that the second one practised witchcraft. I'm not sure if any of this was true. In his later years, when narrating his tales to his grandchildren, my father said that his first wife was a cousin whom he was forced to marry at an early age. He said that he was young and ambitious and not ready to settle down, so after three children the marriage fell apart.

My mother, too, was married before she met Dad and she brought four daughters into the family. I was the eldest child of the five who my parents had when they got married. I also heard that after I was born, my father didn't want any more children. But my mother wanted sons. She already had five daughters. A son in our culture was considered an asset; he was expected to carry the family name, become a provider and take care of the extended family when he was older. My mother felt bad that her husband had sons from his two previous marriages. After my young brother Peter was born, she decided to try again. It was only after the third attempt that she finally got another son and decided that was it.

We were fifteen children! But we didn't all grow up together. Some were young adults and already married when I was born and others, in their late teens, moved out to live with relatives, although my grandmother told me that they had actually run away from home. She said that my father was too strict for the good of any child.

There was always a buzz around the house, people popping in and out and engaging in different activities. A big extended family was common then. There were stepsisters and -brothers, aunts and uncles, cousins and sometimes friends, all living together. Some came to visit and others lived with us. It was often a dysfunctional home, with squabbles, gossip, fights and backbiting.

There was also a lot to do at home. Some fed the dog, others washed the family car; the girls took turns to cook, a chore which was much detested due to the large size of the family. Two people were on cooking duty each day. One would prepare meals for the men and boys, and the other for the women, girls and young children.

Then there was the daily housework. When the girls returned from school or were on holiday, we would assist in washing dishes, laundry and tidying up - this despite there being two domestic workers. The boys would help the gardener to cut the lawn and keep the surroundings clean. My mother believed that children needed to do house work so that they could learn good skills for their future.

For some reason, I was often spared domestic responsibilities. When I was old enough to take turns in cooking and other chores, my father insisted that I shouldn't. This irked my mother who was concerned that I was being spoilt. She said that I would grow up to be irresponsible. "You are messing up this child. She won't get married. Which man would want a woman who does not know how to cook and do housework?" she'd bitterly complain to my father.

But I later proved her wrong because I turned out to be a very good cook and a responsible mother, thanks to the valuable time I spent with both my grandmothers during holidays. I preferred to do domestic chores there than at my parents' home, even if it meant cooking on firewood when I visited Granny in the village.

In no time, I earned myself the nickname 'the special one'. My siblings resented me for being the pet child. But even my mother could not resist pampering me at times. I was a star student; always did my homework, and got good grades at school. I was meticulous and my parents made an example of me.

I was also a shy little girl and to survive the resentment and bullying from older siblings I had to assert myself. I would fight against any verbal attack and would present my case with strong vigour to ensure that I was listened to. I developed the habit of reporting on others to get attention. Anyone who broke the rules, such as eating snacks between meals, secretly sneaking out to a party, splashing the hosepipe on the dog, would be reported on. I did the same at school. They began to call me 'the reporter'.

I sharpened my unorthodox reporting skills so much that one of my teachers suggested that I should become a news reporter when I grew older. My desire to be the centre of attention led me to speak often in front of the class and on behalf of the school during public events. At home, I gave speeches after dinner to those who cared to listen, mainly my mum and dad and our dog, Kimba. It was not the substance of what I said, but the confidence with which I said it, that earned me the admiration of even the siblings who hated my guts. Soon it was realised that I was a good public speaker.

Vivid Childhood Memories

I was five years old when I first flew on an airplane. It was in June, 1972. My memories of walking to board the Zambia Airways plane are vivid. It was a lovely sunny day and we were flying to Nairobi, Kenya. My father held my hand and carried my young sister, Martha in his other arm.

He had just resigned his post as news editor of the Times of Zambia and was going to work in Nairobi as director of communications for the All African Conference of Churches (AACC). I remember him talking about the job with my mother when it was offered to him and she encouraged him to take it. "It would be wonderful for us to live abroad," she said. Kenya was one of the most affluent African countries in the 1970s and going there was a privilege. People rarely travelled out of Zambia back then. Those who did, went to London, the former Soviet Union, East European countries, America, Kenya or Addis Ababa, the latter frequented by my father as a journalist and presidential media adviser, for meetings of the then Organisation of African Unity (OAU).

I would cry each time my father went on a trip abroad. He travelled a lot. I was 'Daddy's girl' and wanted to go with him. He assured me that one day when I was older I, too, would travel around the world. This seemed far-fetched. Now my whole family was soon to embark on our first ever trip outside the country. I didn't understand what it entailed until the day we were all marched to the health clinic to get vaccinated. It was a requirement for our travel. I hated injections and begged the nurse to spare me. I promised I'd stop bullying my young brother and would eat all my food. But my pleas were of no use. "You cannot get onto the plane if you don't get an injection," my mother told me.

On the day of travel, I was excited but nervous. I remember telling my big white doll as we boarded the aircraft that she should not be afraid. In truth, this was a way of self-assurance that my first ever trip abroad would be, to use the pun, 'plain sailing'.

Our family of nine took up most of the economy class cabin. There was my elder brother, Dick and teenage stepsisters, Ethel and Priscilla. My mother sat with baby, Grace who was only a month old, on her lap; while my young brother, Peter and sister, Martha, who seemed to have a passion for crying, sat next to my dad.

Martha cried all the time. She was feeble, petite and meek. She needed attention because she was always sickly. I didn't know what was wrong with her and thought that she faked illness. I hated it when she got all the attention because I felt I was the only one entitled to it. I used to pinch her when no one was looking. But it only made things worse. She'd scream and cry out loudly and I in turn would have my ears pulled or my cheeks pinched by my mother. Luckily, Martha didn't cry on the plane, perhaps because she sat next to my dad. I sat with Dick, aged 15, and each time I turned to look at him he'd stick his tongue out at me. This was his silent way of telling me to face the other way.

I cannot recall much else about the flight except for the sweets and the goodie bags which Peter and I got from the cabin attendants, who were called air hostesses in those days. As always, I bullied Peter into giving me some of his sweets. My trick was to make him believe that if he shared his, he'd grow stronger and taller than I. It worked! I was already short; in fact, I turned out to be the shortest in my family!

In Kenya, my parents entertained a lot at home. We had diplomats, government officials and other people over for dinner parties. I remember our female guests in fancy clothes, glittering jewellery and smelling very nice. I said to myself that I wanted to be like them when I was older. It was a rule that children were not to be seen or heard when there were guests. We'd all be sent to bed if it was in the evening. Peter and I used to sneak out of bed and go to my parents' room where we would re-enact the scene downstairs. There were dos and don'ts in the manner in which we spoke, how we sat in the lounge or at the dining table, how we used cutlery, and other etiquette. My parents insisted on us being proper and polished. My older siblings made a big joke out of all this. As teenagers, they preferred the informal way of life.

Memories of life in Nairobi are scant, but I remember my first day at school. I had heard a lot about school from my sisters. I looked forward to wearing a school uniform and carrying a book bag. When my day came, my mother insisted that I wear a nappy. She wasn't confident that I would know how to ask for the toilet. I spoke very little English. The nursery teacher at Kilimani Primary School where my elder sisters attended, also suggested it best I wear a nappy for the first few days until I was sure of myself. Dick laughed at me all the way to school. He said I was a big baby.

Dick always picked on me. He teased me and knocked his knuckles on my forehead if I tried to fight back. I, in turn, took pleasure in reporting him to my dad at the dinner table, often on trumped up charges such as having seen him chewing gum during the day. Chewing gum was forbidden. My father said it was 'common' and made us look like goats. We would be punished if we were caught doing so both at home and at school, where it was also not allowed.

My first memory of class was the smell of wax crayons. To this day, each time I smell them I am reminded of my first morning at school. As soon as I was introduced, a little white girl stood up from where she was drawing and called me to play. She said she would be my best friend. I cannot remember her name but we played a lot that day.

In no time I was the centre of attraction in my nursery class. I would stand in front of my little classmates and tell stories, in IciBemba, mixed with a bit of English. I would talk about my parents, our dog Kimba, my brother, Dick and many other tales. What mattered to me was the ovation after my speech. It made me feel important and valued. I was already used to doing this at home. In the afternoon, when my elder sister fetched me from class my teacher would recount how I had entertained them with singing and stories, although they did not understand most of what I had said.

My parents were very strict, in fact too strict. They did not allow their teenage children to go out. If they went to parties, it was only those whose invitations came from the parents whom my father knew. My sisters complained about being left out at school because of missing social events. One day they made a plan. They wanted to spend the afternoon at their friend's place but knew that my father would not allow it. So they lied that there was a swimming competition at school. Their plan was to sneak out and walk to their friend's house as soon as Dad had dropped them off. It was not far from the school. Unluckily for them Dad insisted on finding out more about the gala from the headmaster, only to be told that there was none. My poor sisters were exposed.

I will never forget the beating they got that day. Dad drove them to a nearby forest. As he parked the car, Ethel the older one opened her door and ran out. He stopped the car and ran after her. She did not know that her father was a champion sprinter and in no time he caught up with her. He took his belt off and whipped her. The other sister, Priscilla sat crying in the car as did my mother, too scared to get out and stop my dad lest he turn his wrath on her. Then he pulled Priscilla out of the car as Ethel lay on the ground weeping, broke a small branch from a nearby tree and whipped her until the stick was in pieces. He bundled them both into the car and drove home. At the dinner table, he made an example of the two girls explaining how no child of his would ever lie to him. For the first time in my life I hated my father.

Life went on with the same routine: school, work, holidays, dinner parties and holiday trips in Nairobi and around Kenya. Then one day my mother said we had to pack up because we were going back home. It was just over two years since we had arrived in the country.

There was excitement in the family because my father said that he had received a call from home about a plan to appoint him as ambassador to Washington or to the UN Permanent Mission in New York. "It is about time you were recognised for your contribution to your country," my mother told my dad.

My father had been a freedom fighter. He told us stories and showed photographs of the role he and others played in liberating Zambia from British colonial rule. Some stories were heart breaking. Like the ones when he spent time in prison, or was beaten and lost almost everything he had, during fighting between the African National Congress (ANC) of Harry Mwaanga Nkumbula and the splinter United National Independent Party (UNIP) formed by Kenneth Kaunda. My father was a firebrand young man and his heroic tales of struggle and survival were truly inspirational to me even at an early age.

As elsewhere in Africa, the years after the Second World War saw a surge in nationalism and self-assertiveness among the African population. In 1948, Mr Harry Nkumbula, a vibrant freedom fighter, reformed what was known as the Federation of African Welfare Societies and changed the name to the Northern Rhodesia African Nationalist Congress (ANC). 1953 saw the creation of the Federation, comprising Northern Rhodesia (Zambia), Southern Rhodesia (Zimbabwe) and Nyasaland (Malawi). A new constitution introduced by the colonial government in 1958 exposed the divisions that existed in the ANC. When Mr Nkumbula accepted the constitution, younger and more militant members broke away to form the Zambia African National Congress, under the leadership of the ANC Secretary General, Kenneth Kaunda. This radical organization was quickly banned and Kaunda was detained. On his release in 1960, Kaunda assumed leadership of the United National Independence Party (UNIP) and began campaigning vigorously for independence with the critical support of the trade union movement. There was intense rivalry and conflict between ANC and UNIP supporters.

There were recriminations against members of UNIP who had split from the ANC. Party-sponsored thugs pursued my father and others for days to try to kill them. He was a vibrant young member of UNIP in Chifubu constituency, Ndola, where he was billed to run as a member of parliament. His opponents knew he was popular and they wanted to get rid of him. They also accused him of murdering one of their colleagues and were baying for his blood

Men, whom my father suspected were from the ANC, showed up at his house at night but he fled after hiding Dick and his mother, who was my dad's first wife, under a banana tree not too far from the house. They spent the whole night there, as they watched their house and all its possessions burn. Only a few items survived, among them the novel 'Great Expectations' by Charles Dickens, which my father later gave to me as a gift; part of its cover was burned from the fire.

The militant gang chased my father with clubs, sticks and pangas. They got hold of him and began to beat him. The directive was that all UNIP 'traitors' be taught a lesson. My dad swiftly unbuttoned his shirt, took it off and bolted. They were left with his shirt in their hands. He was a sharp sprinter so catching up with him was not an easy feat. By nightfall, he was already badly beaten and needed medical care. He checked into Ndola Central Hospital. There had been a lot of violence in the town that day and hospital wards were full. My father's wounds were nursed and he was given some medicine and admitted for observation. That same night they brought a very sick elderly man into the ward where my father was admitted. There was no bed so they laid him on the floor. My father offered his bed to the old man and the nurses supported the swopping around. He said that he was a young man and could sleep on the floor. His plan after all was to get some rest, then rise early in the morning and flee. He knew that they would come looking for him. But word reached his enemies that my dad was in hospital. Someone was instructed to go there and kill him.

As my father lay on the hospital floor, he heard a doctor and another man whispering as they walked into the ward. The doctor said he knew the bed where my father was. They tiptoed to the bed and an injection was administered to its occupant, who went into a vicious fit and within a few minutes was dead. My father lay still on the floor as all this happened. Convinced that the man whom they thought my father was dead, they quickly left the ward. As soon as they were out of sight, my father got up from the floor, grabbed the shirt from the man who had just been killed and fled the hospital. That night an innocent old man died in place of my father.

This is just one of the many liberation struggle stories my father told me when I was young. I was politicised at an early age. Unlike my older siblings, I took a keen interest in Zambian and world politics and interpreted things from my own childish perspective. I believed that I would one day take part in politics. Thus when I heard my mother say it was time my father was recognised for his contribution, I felt she was justified.

In no time, we were back in Zambia: all of us, except for Dick who was left at boarding school to complete his high school education. Because we were a big family being housed at a Lusaka hotel at the expense of the State, my elder sisters were sent to stay with relatives. "It will only be for a few weeks as we prepare to move to the US," said my mother. We were all excited about our next mission.

But days went by without a word on our next mission. My father made an appointment to see the relevant authorities at State House and he was told to wait; the waiting went from days to weeks. Anxious, my father took another trip to State House. He wanted to speak to the president himself.

This time, my poor dad could not even enter the premises. They told him to go back and that they would contact him when they were ready.

It was two months after we had returned from Nairobi. Life in the hotel had become unbearable for the family. Besides, my father was running out of money. The State had stopped paying our bills under instructions from someone. No one knew exactly who. Desperate, my father went to make another attempt to find out about his so-called appointment. He found nothing.

Then he got a tip-off from a friend in the intelligence network that someone had falsified information about him having worked with external forces while in Nairobi so that he could go back to run for high office. The family realised my father was tricked into quitting his expatriate job in Kenya on the pretext of getting a political appointment, only to be brought back to Zambia to suffer. This was devastating news. I remember hearing my father say, "Why don't they arrest me, if I've done something wrong? I am not afraid of prison?" I was seven years old but felt my blood boil. I was young and helpless. I swore that I would get my way one day.

We moved out of the hotel and stayed briefly with a relative. My father was blacklisted and could not get a job. All his so-called friends abandoned him. None of them dared risk associating with him. He became desperate and destitute with a big family to support. His friends in Kenya offered to pay for my brother's high school education and subsequent university studies. My father believed that if Dick was well educated he would share in his political battles.

We moved to Kitwe on the Copperbelt to stay with my stepsister Jane. She was married to a train driver at Zambia Railways and lived on a modest income. Jane and my mother hated each other, so keeping us in her house gave Jane a good reason to gloat. But my poor mother had nowhere else to go.

Life in my sister's home was tough. I enjoyed playing with children in nearby Ndeke compound. My sister, Priscilla and I slept on the floor in the sitting room. We shared a blanket and fought over who got the biggest part of it. The bottom of the front door of the house had been eaten by rats, so cold winds blew in at night and we had to stop it with newspapers. I hated the nights because we heard sounds of drumming and singing outside. Priscilla said it was witches casting a spell on us. I was terrified. I'd never seen a witch before, except the ones I read about in my fairy tale books. I imagined one in black clothes, with a big ugly nose, outside our door with a broomstick and a big pot of evil things, casting a bad spell. I wanted to go back to Nairobi. I cried every night.

One day my sister, Jane had an argument with her husband after he came home late from a drinking spree. She always bragged to him about her well-to-do father. That night she chided him about how he was just a useless train driver. "My father is a millionaire," said my foolish sister.

"Oh really!" said her husband. "If he is a millionaire then what is he doing under my roof now, and why don't you go to him right this minute?" The arguing went on through the night. My parents were humiliated and angry with my sister. They were left with no choice but to leave.

The following week, we moved to Ndola. My father's cousin Mr Simon Greenwood heard about our predicament. He and other family members contributed money to rent a small house for us. They also donated food and clothes. By now most of my clothes were becoming too small. None of us went to school. My father couldn't afford it.

The house in Northrise was empty but felt homely. Our furniture was left behind in Nairobi. My father had planned to ship everything to Lusaka, but now he had no means of doing so. His friend sent over some items addressed to Mr Greenwood. If the consignment had been addressed to my father, it would have probably been confiscated by the state, Mum had said.

We were so desperately poor that I remember my mother chopping up for firewood the fine oak dining table and chairs which had been sent to Zambia when we returned. We could not afford charcoal all the time and my father felt that his cousins were already doing enough for us. They, too, had meagre jobs so he did not want to be a bother. We had no electricity either, but were just glad to be under our own roof.

It was always a pleasure at the end of the month to see Uncle Simon and his wife Charlotte; they brought us boxes of food. The Greenwoods were mixed race from Cape Town or 'Cape coloureds' as we called them then. Uncle Amos' father was my grandmother's brother. He had gone off to

South Africa where he married a woman of mixed race in Cape Town. The name Greenwood came from the white South Africans whom he worked for as a chef, because he told them that his hometown was green and had a lot of vegetation. So they coined Greenwood as his last name.

Soon it was decided that I should go to school. I started Grade One in 1974 at the aptly named Perseverance Primary School, in Ndola. It was a huge climb down from the posh and more affluent Kilimani School in Nairobi where I had also done a part of my Grade One. But I had to repeat due to missing out on school. I liked school and was determined to learn. My strong educational foundation in Kenya saw me to the top of the class. In no time I was appointed class captain. There were much older children, some as old as nine, but they battled in class; they could not read or write. I recall going through a *Mulenga and Jelita* book in one reading – in less than ten minutes. It took some of my classmates two weeks to master it all.

I used to walk to school. It was not a very long distance from home. I attended class in the afternoon because my mother wanted to ensure that I ate lunch before going to school. Class started at midday. There was no other food for me to pack. We never ever talked about the lunch box. Bread was a luxury and we had it for breakfast whenever it was available.

We ate porridge, nshima and beans, fish or vegetables almost every day. Occasionally at the month end, we would have meat or chicken.

I remember how one day we ran out of almost everything. We only had beans. My mother boiled some so that I could eat before going to school. Then she realised that the firewood had run out and the beans were only half cooked. She poured some into a bowl and suggested that I take a few spoons to give me enough energy to walk to school and concentrate in class. I was so hungry that I enjoyed the uncooked beans. To this day, the smell and taste of half cooked beans brings back very significant memories.

I was often hungry at school and couldn't wait to get back home to take part in the family meal. When our goods were shipped in from Kenya, my mother sold almost everything to buy food. We were left with only three beds and the wooden items which she chopped up for firewood.

The only thing that was spared was my father's radio on which he listened to the BBC World Service or the External Service of Radio RSA on the shortwave frequency. Radio RSA was the propaganda channel of the apartheid government in South Africa. It was established in May, 1966 and closed in 1992. It broadcast messages in English, Portuguese, French, Chichewa and Swahili, to defend the apartheid regime and undermine the impact of liberation movements in southern Africa. These messages were targeted at South Africans in exile. My father reacted angrily to the broadcasts, calling the white government 'a bunch of dirty pigs'.

After the English news on Radio Zambia, Dad would tune into the Chichewa service of Radio RSA, before switching dials to the BBC World Service. I was fascinated by this. I used to sit with him in the living room under candlelight to listen. During the day, he would remove the batteries from the radio and place them out in the sun so that they would be strong enough for the evening broadcasts. I didn't comprehend half of what was said in the news. My father would explain to me and I started taking a keen interest in news and current affairs.

Life went on like that for a while and we got used to it. My father would go out during the day to look for money or to find a job. But he always came back empty handed. I remember hearing my mother cry in the bedroom when my father was not around.

Then one day I heard cheers and laughter from my parents. Dad had been offered a senior job at the Zambia Information Services (ZIS). He was not sure how that appointment came about, considering that he'd been blacklisted, but he was glad anyway.

We moved back to Lusaka into a three-bedroomed furnished government house near the Shorthorn television transmitters in the west of the city. The new job came with a driver and a few perks. The ZIS offices were in a small building near Mulungushi House. My father quickly found a school place for Priscilla and me at Mumuni Primary School, not too far from his office. He said this was a temporary and convenient arrangement until he had settled in his job. He was to move us to what he termed 'a better school'.

Most of the children in my school spoke Chinyanja. I went back to Grade One. My parents thought that was the best after having interrupted my schooling. Priscilla was very smart. She repeated Grade Six and was in no time a key member of the netball team. We hated the school. The playground was dusty and the toilets dirty. Some children bullied me. They said I was a *muzungu*, a white girl, in reference to my fair complexion and good command of the English language. They also threatened to beat me up. Luckily, I had my elder sister for protection.

After school, Priscilla and I used to walk to my dad's office to wait for him to knock off so that we could drive home together. I always looked forward to the afternoons at his office. He'd give us twenty ngwee to buy food at the nearby caravan. Then Priscilla would do her homework in the small library while I'd have a go at the typewriter, or ask the secretary, Mrs Davies a lot of questions. I disturbed her every day.

One day she came up with a plan. She was going to teach me how to knit. She brought wool and knitting needles and spent one afternoon giving me lessons. I enjoyed my new skill so much that I never disturbed her again. She didn't allow me to take the wool home. She kept it in her drawer and immediately I walked into her office, she'd send me to Dad to announce my arrival, then give me a chair in a corner to knit until it was time to go home.

In 1977 we moved from Lusaka West to Jesmondine, a much nicer residential area, but we didn't stay there long. By then my father had been appointed public relations manager at the agricultural parastatal, NAMBOARD, which stood for National Agriculture Marketing Board. Former president, Rupiah Banda was the general manager. But my father had a difficult time, with the suspicion that someone was trying to kill him due to a work-related matter. He blamed it on one of his superiors who wanted him out of the job in order to replace him with a relative. They couldn't find cause to fire him, my father said, so 'knocking him off' was the next option. For almost two weeks, 'thieves' tried to break into our house. My father's assertion was that they were there not to steal but to murder him.

One night, his instinct made him lie in wait for the robbers. My two cousins and our gardener waited up with him. Past midnight, a white van pulled up in front of our gate. The men used an object to break open the lock and slowly drove in. They were four, two seated in front and two in the open back. Without thinking Dad opened the door of the house, forgot to collect his pistol which was on the table and instead grabbed a garden fork, which he had readily prepared for battle.

Throwing caution to the wind, he walked towards the approaching vehicle and smashed the windscreen with the huge garden fork. The other three on his team ran behind him with shovels and pangas. They were ready for war. The thugs at the back of the van jumped out and ran off. The third man also fled, leaving behind the driver, who was almost blinded by the pieces of broken glass from the windscreen. My father pulled him out of the car, threw him to the ground and smashed his head with the fork. He was severely beaten. He managed to stumble along and escape and I understand he was picked up by police who were called in by my father. We never knew what became of him, though I doubt he survived the vicious thrashing.

One would have thought that this should have sent a message to his enemies, but no. A few days later, my father received threatening phone calls. He was now certain that the so-called thieves were in fact bandits, hired by someone to kill him. His response to the calls, 'bring it on!' He promised he'd kill them all before he finally dropped dead. They never bothered him again.

It was decided that we should move house. I quickly made friends with two expatriate children, Vibeke and her brother Harvel who stayed in our new neighbourhood. Their father was a diplomat with the Norwegian Embassy. I played with Vibeke every day. We used to climb trees, play with toys or chase the boys - my brother and hers - around the house. I sometimes tore my dress from the branches in the tree and had a lot of scratches on my legs - earning me a spanking from my mom. But I'd go back and do the same thing repeatedly. Vibeke and I were like hand in glove. Hardly a day went by without us seeing each other. This brought our families close. My mother and hers would go shopping together and share recipes and knitting patterns.

Life was back to normal. My mother did not cry secretly anymore. I knew that she was happy. We had drivers to take us around and my father bought his own car. He also bought my mother a car for her birthday, a Fiat

125. She bragged to her sister that her car had five and not four gears. My mother was always in competition with her sister, Aunt Edna, who was married to a tycoon. They owned a big supermarket and other businesses on the Copperbelt. When our family went to Kenya, they sent their children to England. My mother said that they copied what we did, out of envy. But my mother always said a lot of things! The rivalry between the two sisters went on until they died, Aunt Edna in 1999 and my mother in 2004.

I left Mumuni for a new school which I enjoyed. In no time, I became the teacher's pet. Miss Simasiku at Northmead Primary School had a profound influence on my early life. She was young, energetic and pleasant. She also helped me with my speeches and taught me public speaking skills. She instilled confidence in me. My first ever prize at school was a coffee mug, which I got for my part in a school play, enacting the birth of Jesus Christ.

One good thing led to another. After two years, my father, an ardent journalist, went back to his profession, lecturing in various journalism subjects at the Evelyn Hone College in Lusaka. With the stability and improved lifestyle came the other dependents – the extended family. We always had relatives staying with us; the house was ever crowded.

I disliked crowds. I have always been a private person. My father seemed to pay more attention to his nephews than his own children, so said Mum, and it riled her. She became bitter and resentful. There were arguments and fights, gossip and all sorts of problems. When one family member left, another or two would come forth. I would withdraw to my room which I shared with my two sisters, lock myself in and read. I missed Vibeke a lot. I heard that her family moved back to Norway a few months after we moved house. I wanted to stay in touch but didn't know how. Our parents also lost contact.

As seasons changed, so did our lives. Priscilla passed her Grade Seven and went to boarding school. Dick completed his university studies and was back in Zambia working for the meteorological department. He had a small house in the Chelston police camp which he shared with his policewoman girlfriend, Irene. I'd go there sometimes to escape our rowdy home.

In 1978, when I was eleven years old my mother decided it best to send me to an all-girls school. I moved to Lusaka Girls Primary School. Before long, my teacher suggested I skip one grade and go to the seventh; she was sure that I would cope.

I didn't have many friends at school. I found a lot of the girls unambitious and boring. My goal was to be a television presenter and they thought I was crazy. They teased me and laughed at me. Leap-frogging to Grade Seven brought on other challenges. The girls were much older.

A bully called Joyce utterly detested me. She had failed twice. This was her third attempt at getting into secondary school. During class breaks she ordered me around and threatened to beat me and other younger girls if we did not give her food. She never carried a lunch box or any money for the tuck shop, which was normal among school children. No one really knew her age but some said she must have been fifteen or sixteen. I was only twelve. She was very dull and paid no attention in class. In our maths test she got 2%. No one dared laugh at her. I giggled. I was not afraid of her; being bullied was not new to me. I was bullied at home and was good at fighting back.

Losing Viyembo

Viyembo was a loud, scruffy, carefree girl. She lived in the backyard quarters with her parents and brother Mudala. Her father worked as a gardener. Although she was ten years old, Viyembo did not go to school. The excuse was that her parents didn't have enough money for her education. My mother offered to pay for Viyembo's schooling but her parents turned it down. It was discovered later that the reason was because her mother wanted her to stay at home and do the housework. Mudala went to school.

Viyembo's mother sold home-made beer at a tavern in a nearby township. She came back home very drunk every night. My mum joked that she probably drank more beer than she actually sold. It was not clear whether she made any profit from her business, but she clearly was contented, for she sang out loudly and happily all the way home from the tavern. My father would have to get up late at night to open the gate for her. She would stagger past him singing, oblivious of the inconvenience she was causing her husband's employer.

The gardener was cautioned frequently to control his wife or they'd be replaced, but nothing changed. I didn't want them to go. I liked Viyembo. She was my good friend and I played with her every day after school. My parents discouraged me, saying the gardener's child had bad manners, did not bathe and could infect me with lice or scabies. But the fun I derived from playing with her outweighed the threat of catching her germs.

One day, Viyembo asked me to accompany her to buy a few groceries in Mtendere, the township where her mother sold alcohol. I had never been there before and was excited to go. Mum allowed me on condition that I came back home before my father returned from work. He would be very angry to hear that his daughter had gone with the gardener's child whom he despised.

"Please be careful with cars on the road and don't talk to strangers," my mother cautioned. I was nine years old and still learning to cross the road.

Viyembo suggested we take a footpath in the bush because it was shorter and would keep us away from the traffic. We stopped to play, pick flowers and grass, chase one another and have a good laugh. We also played a lot on our way back. The sun was beginning to set and I remembered that I had to get home before my father did. We raced back and just about managed to get through the gate before Dad drove in. Mum was terrified.

My friendship with Viyembo grew stronger. I shared my toys, clothes, food and sweets with her. I insisted that Viyembo go along whenever we visited family and friends. Viyembo soon filled the gap left by Vibeke, my Norwegian friend. She also became part of the family. She spent more time in the main house than in the small backyard quarters. My mother would invite her to take a bath when I was at school, to ensure that she was clean and would not 'infect me with disease'.

On one cold winter's night Viyembo's mother came back drunk as usual. A few minutes after she got home, her husband knocked on our front door to ask if their daughter was with us. They said she had not come home, although she was last seen in the early evening at the tavern with her mother. But Viyembo was not with me that night.

Soon police were called in and a search party began looking for her. They retraced her steps back to where she was last seen. It was the early hours of the morning and no one was at the tavern. They called her name. Viyembo was nowhere to be found. I was frightened and wondered what had happened to my best friend.

The next day my Dad drove with her parents to a few relatives staying in Lusaka, with the hope that she had gone to one of them. They still did not find her. After searching for nearly a week, my mother felt obliged to reveal to Dad that I had recently accompanied Viyembo to the township using a shortcut in the bush. She had no choice but to let out this secret in the hope that any information could lead to finding the missing child. By now, they were almost certain that something bad had happened to her.

I was roped in to provide information about the route I had taken with my friend. It was not a frequently used path. The search yielded nothing. The following day my father, police and Viyembo's parents decided to go back to the same bush and extend the search.

In less than an hour, they came back home. Viyembo's mother was crying loudly. And soon my mother began to cry too. They had found the decomposed body in the bushes. Viyembo had been murdered in a ritual killing in which her heart and private parts had been removed.

26

Soon there was a funeral. People were mourning; my mother was particularly traumatised at the thought that the child was murdered in the same bush area in which I had been only a few days earlier. I couldn't sleep at night, nor concentrate at school. I worried that the people who had killed Viyembo would come looking for me and do the same. I hardly stepped out of the house. At night I would wake up screaming and run to my parents' room, frightened that someone was trying to steal me. I began to bite my nails. I also started wetting the bed and did so for weeks. My brothers and sisters teased me and told the whole neighbourhood about it. This hurt me even more.

Every morning I would wake up thinking that my friend would show up to play. I missed her a lot. Initially I didn't understand it all. No one close to me had died before so I was confused. In those days, deaths were few and far apart. Children did not know what it meant. I took comfort in my mother's story that Viyembo was now in heaven and that she had turned into a little angel who was now watching over me. This helped me to get over the loss but I never forgot my loud, dirty, rough best friend.

Then a very Scary Experience

For several years after Viyembo was murdered, Zambia went through a very bad patch - women and young children were kidnapped, raped and then murdered for their body parts. Parents were on guard. We were not allowed to move about unaccompanied. Children had to stay in groups, with their parents or a responsible adult.

One day my parents did not pick me up from Lusaka Girls Primary School. My father thought that Mum would fetch me and she thought he would do so after work. He got home around 7 p.m. to discover that I was not back yet. They panicked. Soon a search party involving my parents, the police, neighbours and other family members was in action, looking for me.

In the meantime, I was waiting outside the school because the gate had been locked. I was crying and terrified. This had never happened to me before. I thought something terrible had happened to my parents. I heard men's voices approaching so I jumped into a nearby ditch to hide. After they had passed I decided it was not safe to stand outside the school gate. I had to get help. I ran to a residential block not too far from the school and knocked on the first door. No one answered. I went to the next house. A lady opened the door. I explained to her that my parents had not picked me up from school, I was frightened and I wondered if she had a phone I could use to tell them where I was. I was sure that they had been to the school by now and did not find me. She was not helpful. She shook her head, said "No," and then shut the door in my face. I cried out loudly. I didn't know where to go.

The area behind Lusaka Girls Primary School was not as well developed and lit up as it is today. In 1978, it was surrounded by bush. Taking one step away from the housing block meant a step into danger. But I was determined that my parents find me. Memories of how my friend went missing, how they searched for her for days before they picked up her body haunted me. Was the same to happen to me?

I was now wailing loudly as I ran down the road, not sure where to go. Suddenly I saw a man approaching. When he walked towards me, I bolted. I thought he was 'one of them'. He ran after me and begged me to stop. He said he had recognised my uniform. I was from his school and he

29

wanted to help me. Suddenly I, too, realised that his voice was familiar. He was the deputy headmaster. I stopped and told him what had happened. He suggested I spend a night at his house which was close by, then he would take me to school in the morning where my parents would find me. At first I thought it was a good idea. I was extremely scared and just wanted to be off the dangerous dark streets. It was nearly 10 p.m.

But when we go to his house I began to cry. I wanted to go home. He said he had no car and no phone at home to call my family. Because of the security situation taxis did not operate at night. I was worried that if I spent a night at his house, my parents would die of sorrow.

Then a thought occurred to me. I remembered that there was a hotel down the road. I didn't know the name, but perhaps if he took me there my parents would find me. So reluctantly he and his wife walked me to the Intercontinental Hotel. Immediately I walked through the main entrance, I sighed with relief. The bright lights, warmth and sound of the piano playing in the background assured me that I would be safe.

The hotel staff were very helpful. We did not have a phone at home so they called our neighbour to tell them where I was. They also rang a few police stations in Lusaka to inform them, in case my parents went there to look for me, that I was safe and sound at the hotel. In no time, my parents were there to pick me up and I was back home. I hold a special place in my heart for the Intercontinental Hotel.

Dancing on the Drums

It was a school holiday and I looked forward to it. At least twice a year, my brother and I spent a few days at my father's village in Serenje, six hours drive from the city. We enjoyed the countryside. Being there meant fewer restrictions from what we were accustomed to back home.

I first went to the village when I was a baby. My parents took me there to show me to my grandmother and other relatives, particularly Chief Serenje, because I bear the name Mumbi, the tribe's ancestor.

When I went back years later, I despised everything about the place - mud huts, no running water, no electricity and certainly no television. During a visit one day, I woke up to find my parents had gone. They had left before dawn. I cried my heart out, thinking I had been abandoned to life in the bush forever. "How will I cope in this place? I don't have friends, they don't speak English, the food tastes funny and there are no proper toilets," I lamented. My grandmother was concerned that I would fall ill from the crying. She comforted me that my parents would return in two days to pick me up. The truth was I was to spend more than three weeks there.

I eventually settled in and began to enjoy myself. I would join my peers to fetch water from the river, collect firewood, pound maize, grind millet and even cook - chores which I didn't do back home. I preferred housework at my grandmother's to housework in the city. I found it more exciting. I was later to learn that my being abandoned in the village was my mother's plan to ensure that I was raised like a 'proper African girl' by getting acquainted with our traditional customs. There was no 'daddy' here, to protect me.

Night-time was different though. I recalled all the stories I'd heard about lions and hyaenas, witches and ghosts. I feared that they might come into my grandmother's house and take me away to be eaten. I would cuddle up very tightly to Grandma until morning.

This holiday was different. I had just turned fifteen, was a seasoned visitor to the village and fitted in well. Aunt Esnat informed me and two cousins who lived in the village that we were to be taken 'into the house'. I didn't understand what this entailed but looked forward to it.

When in the house, the door was locked with a wooden latch. We changed from our normal clothes into the traditional tassel skirts that had been made for us. Our little budding breasts were left uncovered. In the house were two elderly women, my grandmother and my two aunts.

"Girls, you are in seclusion in this house because you have come of age. This means that you are no longer children but young ladies ready for passage into womanhood," one of the women explained. She went on to say that this was happening because we had reached puberty so we would be locked in for three weeks, to be bathed, fed and groomed into young beautiful women, ready for marriage. We could only go out secretly to use the pit latrine. I thought this was a big joke. We giggled and made funny faces. We were scolded, "You are not allowed to laugh and giggle here. This is serious business."

I had heard stories of how young girls who had come of age were locked in a house for weeks and 'taught'. I had no idea what that meant and was convinced that such would never happen to me.

In no time, my cousins and I had become attentive students. We liked the seclusion because we didn't have to collect firewood, scrub the pots with sand using our bare hands, as aunt Dolika had always insisted, and certainly did not have to pound maize and cassava. What we enjoyed most was feeding time. Food cooked specially for us was brought into the house. Each day came with something new and delicious – fried caterpillars, fresh fish, roasted maize and groundnuts; chicken, beans, a variety of vegetables and game meat. A special clay mixed with herbs was rubbed onto our faces and bodies so that we would look more beautiful after we came out of the house. We would wake up very early in morning before the village folk arose, to take a bath in big basins outside.

Our daily routine involved lessons on personal hygiene, relationship with boys, good conduct and behaviour, domestic science, traditional dances and 'how to please a man'. The lessons were both theoretical and practical. Drums and songs were sung and their meaning interpreted. We were told that this initiation ceremony was to prepare us for what would come years later when we got married.

Details of what happened in the house were to remain confidential. And no one was to see us until our initiation training was over. The reason was that many years ago, girls got married when they reached puberty, usually around fourteen or fifteen years old. They would go through the ceremony to prepare them for marriage. Soon after they came out of the training, there would be a suitor within, or from a nearby village, ready to court or propose.

On the last day of our in-house coaching we were woken up very early. We bathed and dressed in short traditional skirts made of sack cloth. We also had a lot of beads around our necks and waists.

"It is now time to come out," said Aunt Esnat. She told us that the entire village, and others from the neighbourhood, had been gathering since early morning to witness the special ceremony. There was a lot of excitement and I could hear singing and drumming. We were now mature and well trained, and ready to be shown off to the community. Our last task was to stand on top of upturned water drums, and perform a variety of dances in front of the villagers.

I could have died of shame. "Do they expect me to dance in front of all these people? Do they think I am a villager?" I was very upset but recalled the lesson on obedience I'd been taught. I kept quiet and did as I was told.

Finally, the door opened. There was ululating, singing and drumming as we were taken out of the house, our heads covered with traditional cloth. We were helped up onto the water drums. The special music began and my cousins and I danced heartily to the drumming. I spotted my parents in the crowd and almost jumped off to run and hug them. But I remembered what aunt Esnat told me, "You are now grown up and need to maintain a distance from your parents, especially your father, other men and boys, until the right one to marry you comes along."

CUE and CUT…. The start of my TV Career

When I was seven years old, the class teacher asked what we wanted to be when we were older. I raised my hand and said that I was going to be a TV star. My classmates laughed and teased me for months. Back then children aspired to be teachers, doctors, policemen or nurses. They did not perceive working for television. But I was resolute about my ambition. The teasing went on until I left secondary school.

My teenage life, like most young adults, was not easy. Mine was particularly difficult. The boys at school picked on me. I was resented for speaking out in class, getting good grades and even for being too ambitious. They said I was a snob. I was a dominant personality always wanting to be in charge. At home, I had no one to talk to about my pain. They didn't understand me. They thought I was crazy because of what they said was my far-fetched outlook to life. I became reclusive. After school I would sit in my room, do my homework, study and fantasize. I created an imaginary friend with whom I'd chat, laugh and share my dreams. My dream was always to be on TV. I wanted to be a movie star, or a newsreader. I would write TV scripts and act them out with my imaginary friend or get my young brothers and sisters to act some parts. I would sit in front of the mirror and pretend to read the news. I drew a lot of happiness and satisfaction in doing this.

After secondary school, despite my well known public speaking talent, my father suggested I study linguistics. He said I was eloquent and had the flare for languages. I spoke and wrote impeccable English for my age. I also mastered French and other local languages very quickly and spoke them well.

He enrolled me for a Bachelor's Degree in Linguistics at a university in Stuttgart, in West Germany as it was called before the unification in 1991. It was also my father's favourite country. He studied journalism and worked there for a few years before I was born. But I couldn't go to university because my parents failed to raise the funds needed, due to my sister falling ill. Everything was diverted towards her medical care. This devastated me.

Dad suggested I study Mass Communications at the University of Zambia. I didn't stay there for more than a month. I found the lectures boring. Then he enrolled me into the journalism school at the Evelyn Hone College in Lusaka. It was one of the country's most prestigious colleges offering first-class vocational training. He had taught there years before and later went back to head the journalism department. Again, after a few weeks, I decided to leave. I just wanted to be on television.

In early November 1985, I found my way to the national broadcasting station. It was called Zambia Broadcasting Services then. I asked to see the human resource manager. I confidently walked into Mr Mtonga's office and told him that I was there for a TV job.

Mr Mtonga gave me a slow steady look, and calmly told me to go back home. "Young lady, you are really young, immature and totally inexperienced. We do not employ grade seven drop-outs here. All our broadcasters are college or university graduates," he said.

I was heart-broken. I went back home and cried. It was my childhood dream to be on television and I was not a 'grade seven drop-out'. My parents who had not been aware that I had sneaked out to look for a job, soon heard about my visit to the TV station. I was told off. I was stubborn and ambitious. A month later I decided to give the TV job another go. This time, with some research, I found out that the person to see was Mr Charles Mando. "Please give me a chance for an audition. If I do not do well, then I will go away and never come back," I told him. He was impressed by my determination and confidence. He was sure that I was just a little girl obsessed with being on television, so giving me a quick audition to satisfy my curiosity would not hurt. I was nearly eighteen years old, but looked thirteen.

He took me to the TV studio and whispered to the crew to "give the poor little girl a chance to be in front of the camera, even if it does not amount to anything." Also lined up for auditions were more mature and experienced journalists, fresh from college. They scoffed at the naive and inexperienced competition I offered. I was too excited to be intimidated by their polished appearance. After all, I had taken on my much older siblings at home, and won!

When my turn came, I was taken to the seat in front of the camera and given a news script to read. The studio manager comforted me saying that it was okay if I did badly, because I was young and all would understand.

The entire crew in the studio appeared sorry and scared for 'this little girl who had decided to put herself through a very challenging test.'

Then the studio director gave the command; "Cue and Cut" – and I began to read. They held their breath! When I finished reading, they all ran to the desk where I was seated in the studio.

"Young lady, have you ever been on TV before?" the director asked. My audition was so good that they were convinced that I had done TV before. What they didn't know is that for almost ten years, I had sat in front of the mirror every day, and practiced reading the news, thanks to solitude, my favourite companion! I was so accomplished that when the TV camera rolled and I started the audition, some of the crew ran out of the studio to inform others of my level of talent. They were profoundly astonished. Even the bigger girls who had come in for auditions admitted that they were not a match for me.

When it was time to go home, I asked the studio director what Cue and Cut meant. "It means get ready and start speaking because you are now on air," he said, with a pleasant smile on his face.

In the evening, I received a call from Mr Mando. "Hello Maureen Nkandu," the voice said on the other end. "I am phoning to inform you that we were very impressed with your audition this morning. However, you are still very raw and under-age, but we would like to give you a try. Congratulations, you've got the job."

My head spun. I could hardly believe it. For me, doing the audition was an achievement enough. Now I had the job! I was to report for work the following week.

One phrase kept ringing in my head. "'Cue and Cut'. I will be hearing this quite a lot," I thought. That marked the beginning of my illustrious broadcasting career.

Working for ZNBC

My first few weeks at the TV station were filled with childish bliss! Everything was new and exciting. I was happy to meet in person the faces I had seen on the telly. I would spend hours after work narrating to my family what my new workmates looked like, what they said, how they dressed and the goings on at work.

Radio and TV presenters were housed in what was called the General Service office. It was a big, wide open-plan space nicknamed 'the Zoo' because the celebrities were named after animals. The office was also filled with gossip, arguments, back-stabbing, rumours, laughter, tears and a lot of fun. Ms Pauline Tembo, the office secretary known as 'the zoo keeper', ensured sanity and order.

I was the youngest of them all. I took pleasure in being sent to the cafeteria to buy drinks and snacks for my colleagues until my mother told me never to do it again. "You are an employee like the rest of them, so they should not send you around. You are not an office orderly," she said. I stopped it.

My nickname was 'Young Maureen'. I was given the name by former president Kenneth Kaunda, on my first assignment to State House as a reporter. My supervisor assigned me to cover a courtesy call meeting to try out my reporting skills. The Soviet Union's ambassador and a visiting delegation from Moscow were meeting the president. It was my first time at State House and I was mesmerised. Journalists were called into the meeting room to set up their equipment. Soon the Soviet delegation walked in, followed by Dr Kaunda and his security detail. I thought I was dreaming. It was fantastic being in the same room with all the important people. When everyone was seated, Dr Kaunda began to speak; then the head of the Soviet delegation. I sat at the end of the table and stared at everything around me. I admired the well-decorated room, the wall paintings, the exquisite furniture; my eyes moved around the room, I stared at the president, and his security men who looked serious... my mind began to float...

Then I heard Dr Kaunda call me, "Young Maureen, come here. Come and sit here, next to me." There was an empty seat next to him and he beckoned to me to take it. Everyone in the room was quiet, wondering why the powerful leader had interrupted an important meeting to call for my attention.

"What are you doing young Maureen?" he asked.

"Nothing," I answered. There was a soft chuckle in the room.

Then he said, "Look at your friends from the media, what are they doing?"

I stared at them then innocently said "I don't know." The whole room burst into laughter. I was eighteen years old and too naïve to comprehend the seriousness of the occasion.

"They are all taking down notes. They are listening to us and taking notes. Can you see that?" said the president.

"Ooh!" I said. By now everyone in the room was laughing at me, including the Soviet delegation to whom my conversation with the president was being interpreted.

"Do you have a notebook and pen?" Dr Kaunda asked.

"Yes I do. They are in my bag," I answered.

"Okay, take them out and start taking down notes. Write everything I say and everything the others say. When you go back to the TV station, you will report what we said here, based on the notes you will have written," said the president.

This was my first lesson in mainstream reporting, given by the head of state himself!

From then on, each time I went to State House, President Kaunda referred to me as 'Young Maureen' and insisted that I sit next to him and take down notes. That is how I became known affectionately as 'Young Maureen'.

I enjoyed my work as a continuity announcer and occasional reporter. My mentors encouraged me to do more, to go to university and improve my journalistic skill. Two years after joining ZNBC, I got a Diploma in Journalism from the Indian Institute of Mass Communications in New Delhi.

Although I was a good presenter, I was not allowed to read the news. It was the preserve of more experienced presenters who'd been through the mill and carried authority. I nagged my boss to let me read the news. He wouldn't let me. Journalists at ZNBC were well trained, well travelled and exposed to high standards of broadcasting. They had been trained in-house at the BBC, or Radio Deutsche-Welle, or Voice of America and other good international broadcasters. I was fortunate to learn from them.

My break on the news desk came by default. The anchor of the day failed to show up by studio cut off time. They couldn't find a replacement for him. I offered to step in. They had no choice but to let me. I had been to the newsroom to get an extra copy of the bulletin as it was being prepared. I did this all the time when I was on duty. I'd take the copies home and practice news reading. I also wanted to know what was going on before it was broadcast. I read the news like a seasoned anchor that night and was scheduled from then on. I went on to win three ZNBC *Newscaster of the Year Awards* (1989, 1990 and 1991), One Press Association of Zambia *Newscaster of the Year* (1992), and the prestigious *Marang Award* at BOP Television in South Africa (1993) for the *Best TV Personality of the Year!*

Falling in Love

I had now settled into my job. TV audiences fell in love with my youth and naivety. I was in my late teens when I started work, probably the youngest person ever to be employed full-time by the country's only broadcaster. But it was my polished and confident demeanour that they liked. I received dozens of fan letters every day. The switchboard was inundated with calls from people, mostly men, wanting to speak to me or take me out on a date. My fan base increased each day.

At first, I could not deal with the fame. It was overwhelming and not what I'd expected. I complained to my mum about being mobbed at the supermarket and in other public places. People wanted my autograph or just to shake my hand. "That is the price of fame and you must accept and live with it," she said.

My second real test of reporting came after my humiliation at State House, when I was sent to report on the return to the country of a very senior government official. Honourable Grey Zulu was UNIP's secretary general, and his role was equivalent to that of vice president. He was a no-nonsense disciplinarian who had played a part in the liberation struggle of the country. Mr Zulu had gone overseas for an important meeting and I was to interview him about his mission. I had never done such a story before but I was always up to the challenge. In no time, my camera crew and I were at the airport.

The flight landed on time and I carried out my duties as expected. I was now eager to rush back to the office to edit my story and get it ready for broadcast. But the cameraman and the driver did not want to leave right away. They told me that a football team from Europe was on the same flight as Mr Grey Zulu and they wanted to see them.

"So what is so special about these footballers?" I asked, irritated that my colleagues were delaying my work process. "One of our young talented footballers plays for them and he is here at the airport. We want to meet him," said the cameraman. His visiting club from Belgium was to play a game against the country's national team, 'The KK Eleven'.

The two men disappeared and found themselves in the VIP lounge. I tried to drag them out because I was keen to get back to the office to edit my report. As I reached out to tap one on the shoulder, I tripped over a bag and fell. Next to the bag over which I tripped was the young Zambian footballer whom my colleagues had come to greet. His name was Kalusha Bwalya. He was the country's most famous footballer.

Embarrassed, I quickly got up and ran out of the room to wait in the car. When my workmates joined me, they said there was no need to be ashamed. One of them even offered to take me to the footballers' hotel so that I could meet them, to redeem myself. I took up my colleague's offer, but I nearly took off when I saw Kalusha coming. I wanted to meet him but was too shy. Anyway, we were introduced and he said he'd be in touch later. And he did contact me.

One evening after I'd finished reading the news I received a call from the switchboard. "Hello, good evening, this is Kalusha. Is that Maureen?" asked the voice on the other end. I was quite fed up of such phone calls, which normally came in after I'd appeared on TV. Dozens of men called to chat me up. They would ask my age, or if I had a boyfriend. Some were more direct and proposed to marry me.

"Yes, this is she, how can I help you?" He said that he was calling me because he had just seen me on TV, liked the way I presented myself and wanted to say 'well done'. He suggested we meet for a drink one day when I was not too busy. My face turned red. I had mixed emotions of embarrassment, anger, shame and confusion. I responded by saying that I would ask my mum for permission. He went silent for a moment, and then laughed. "You need to get permission from your parents to go out? I thought you were a big girl. How old are you?" he asked.

Kalusha would pick me up from the office, sometimes with his Zambian football teammates Wisdom Chansa and Lucky Msiska. We'd go clubbing, or for dinner and drinks. Then he'd drop me off at home. I began to enjoy my new life. I'd never dated before and this was great fun.

I remember him coming to pick me up from work one evening when my TV shift was over. Kalusha was already at the door of the studio to pick me up when I finished. My workmates were falling over themselves to greet him. I could not understand what all the fuss was about. Some wondered what he was doing at the TV studio so late at night. Even the soldiers at the gate abandoned their posts to meet him. They were utterly shocked when they saw him and me walk hand-in-hand to his rented car. "Wow, is that her boyfriend?" "When did they meet…?" the questions did not stop.

Peering, curious eyes and wagging tongues followed us everywhere we went. It was to be expected. We were a celebrity couple. I remember one day when we walked into the Municipal Sports Club in Lusaka everybody and everything stopped. It was as if people had seen two ghosts. I wanted to run back to the car. Kalusha gripped my hand tightly and whispered, "Take it easy, you'll be fine." Being with him increased the pressure on me. It was hard enough to deal with my own fame; now I had to cope with the double fame. Our relationship became the talk of the town. We had been going public for almost a month when Kalusha decided that he would spare me the torment of public attention. I didn't go home that day. My new boyfriend asked me to stay over. By now I didn't worry about what my parents thought. I was sure I had now been liberated from them.

The following morning as we walked past the lobby, we both heard one hotel staff member whisper, "She was a virgin… there was blood on the linen." I wanted to run home. This was too embarrassing. Kalusha told me to grow up. "Who cares if they know that you were a virgin?" The whole town was awash with the story that I had lost my virginity. Before he returned to Belgium, Kalusha and I visited his family in Mufulira.

All Things Bright and Beautiful

The man who called me the previous day to arrange a meeting, met me in the lobby of the TV station at the appointed time. He introduced himself as Elvis Cumbe, a music promoter and event manager.

Elvis said he wanted to speak to me about entering a beauty contest. I wasn't interested. My sisters said that such contests were for stupid girls with low self-esteem. I was certain that I was neither stupid nor lacked self-esteem. He spoke in a strange accent, and tried to convince me that the main purpose of the contest was to identify a winner who would work on children's charity programmes for a year. He said people had asked him to approach me about entering because my public profile would suit the role of a child ambassador. I later found out that Elvis was a Mozambican national resident in Zambia.

Before then beauty contests in Zambia were banned because it was felt that the act of women parading themselves in swimwear in public was both degrading and uncultured. Elvis told me that the ban had now been lifted and to give authenticity to the contest, the first lady, Madam Betty Kaunda would be the patron of the pageant. He said that is why the phrase 'children's charity', would be added to the Miss Zambia title.

I told my mother about Mr Cumbe's proposal. She encouraged me to go for it. She revealed that she too was once a beauty queen in her hey-days and the face of Pepsi Cola.

I went to Mr Cumbe's office the next day to tell him that I would join the competition. The rules were stiff. The girls were to be single, with no children, not younger than eighteen years and not older than twenty five; no alcohol or smoking was allowed. Importantly, we needed to have a good general knowledge and a passion for children and charity work. I loved children. I phoned Kalusha in Belgium to tell him about my decision. He was not too keen on it and discouraged me, but my mind was made up.

The programme leading to the contest, which was two months away, was rigorous. There were fourteen other contestants. Rehearsals were at least twice a week. I was often tired because I attended in the evening after work and during weekends. I didn't enjoy the sessions. The other girls were unfriendly and spiteful. They said bad things about me, such as I had an unfair advantage because I was on television and had a famous boyfriend. I regretted having gone into it, but I decided to stay on.

A professional modelling coach gave us the drill on how to walk, smile, pose and connect with the audience. I was very uncomfortable modelling in my swimsuit because of scars on my legs, caused by a car accident only a month after I joined ZNBC. But I was told not to worry because I could wear pantyhose to cover them up.

Finally, the day of the contest came. The event was well attended including high level guests such as the patron of the pageant herself. The show was also broadcast live on television. My workmates and others didn't know that I was one of the contestants. Mr Cumbe had suggested we make it a surprise.

There were six judges on the panel and I had to impress them. My mother, a fashion designer, made the three outfits I wore. I had butterflies in my tummy. My competitors were right. I was very popular and people liked me, judging from the loud whistling and applause I got each time I went on stage.

Dinner was served after the catwalk rounds. I could barely eat. When I entered the contest, I did it for the fun of it. Little did I realise how big the whole thing was. There was a lot at stake; a big prize to be won, a trophy, a lot of money and a one year title as Miss Zambia. This role entailed travelling around the country, sometimes in support of charitable causes for children. The enormity of it all became clear when I was on the runway in that packed hotel hall. I had to win or face humiliation as the TV girl who lost a beauty contest. Again, I wished I had never entered.

Finally, the judges made their decision. All the girls lined up on stage. The Master of Ceremonies first announced the third prize winner, then the second place. I was hoping it would be me. If I was not either of the two, and the first place winner was not me, it would be a disaster. But I wasn't in second place either. "Now ladies and gentlemen," said the MC, "the first ever Miss Zambia Children's Charity ..." I could hear my heart beat like a drum. I was so carried away with worrying that I did not hear the MC announce my name. "Maureen you've won, you are the winner, step forward," said one of the girls on stage with me.

I awoke from my few seconds of fearful daydream. "Oh no it's me," I said to myself. I stepped forward, shook the hand of the MC and that of the first lady, who was on stage to present me with the trophy, the glitzy crown and the cheque. It was a beautiful moment for me as the cameras clicked and flashed. I was so happy that I almost cried, but the training taught us to be composed. I sat on the special chair with the two runners-up standing one on each side. This was no doubt one of the best days of my life.

The hard work began a month after I was crowned Miss Zambia. My first assignment was to donate food and clothes to children at the Kasisi Orphanage about thirty kilometres outside the capital city. It was my choice that I begin there. I had heard about the orphanage from my mother. She had prepared me a few times that in case she and my father died, we might end up in the orphanage. I developed a special affection for the children at Kasisi and the handicapped children at Cheshire Homes in Lusaka. I handed them clothes, sweets, biscuits, and gave their caregivers bags of mealie meal, potatoes and other food that had been donated by the wives of diplomats and the expatriate community.

The next big event was a fund-raising show by Zambian artists. My role was to meet and receive the guests. Kalusha was around on holiday and I wanted him to come along for moral support. He was not too keen. He'd cautioned me against going into the competition in the first place and felt that I was demeaning myself.

"People say that girls who win these competitions sleep with the judges. Why are you embarrassing yourself?" Kalusha asked me.

The following day I told Mr Cumbe that I was stepping down from the role because my now fiancé didn't want me to be involved. Elvis advised that doing so would be a bad idea, considering that I was endorsed by the highest office in the land. He suggested that I take a very low profile and phase out quietly when it was time to handover to the next person. Within that year in 1987, I fell pregnant, one of the rules I was not to break. Kalusha was happy, saying this was a good reason for me to step down as Miss Zambia. And I did.

Hanged, Drawn and Quartered - Rumours of the Coloured-Indian Baby

Work was not fun anymore. My boss would call me into his office frequently and try to kiss me. When I resisted, he threatened to fire me. Then there were the politicians, businessmen, footballers, former school mates, colleagues at work and many others. Some said that they wanted me for a wife, a mistress or just for sexual pleasure. A few of them threatened to break up my relationship with Kalusha. I also got phone calls from angry women who accused me of flirting with their husbands. If I was seen in public with any man, I was accused of having an affair with him.

To add to my woes, I was stalked by Chongo Chingungulu, the office orderly, whom it was later discovered had mental problems. Unbeknownst to me, he followed me everywhere I went. He knew where I lived, where I shopped and what I did in my free time. He even knew where my parents stayed. One evening he showed up at their house to ask for my hand in marriage. But it was only after Chongo tried to attack me in the women's toilet, that people realised he was a serious menace.

Things took a turn for the worse when I turned down my boss's dinner invitation. He removed me from reading news and confined me to office work. This affected my morale. I was a front line girl and being in the background was a knock on my self-esteem. I was hurt but couldn't tell anyone the reason for the move. I was afraid to report him in case he became true to his word and fired me.

Then there was the Tanzanian prophet who always appeared from nowhere. He said he had an important message for me. "Things are going to be very bad for you," he warned. He said that he could prevent the calamity if I gave him some new clothes, shoes, a TV set and money. I didn't believe in prophets so I ignored him. He rocked up a few days later with the same message. I threatened to report him to the police. He did not stop. The last straw was when he rocked up just before I boarded a bus to go to work. He told me that I was two months pregnant with a baby girl. "Nice try," I said sarcastically. I told him to get lost. I never saw him again.

Shortly after that, I realised he was right after all. I was pregnant. Delighted at the news, Kalusha was even keener on having me with him. I wanted a fairy tale wedding. He preferred a quiet, private family event.

He cited the tight football training and club league schedules as well as the negative vibes around our relationship, as reasons why we should have a quick, small and unelaborate wedding. By this time, he had already formalised the whole marriage issue with my family.

I obliged. Soon a small traditional process was arranged and I joined him in Brugge, Belgium. We led a fairly good lifestyle although my pregnancy made me often sick. I would watch him train or play club games every week. I got quite homesick. Because I was with child, I stayed home and didn't work, while he trained every day and played league games. He had promised my dad that I would go to university after the baby was born.

What I didn't know was that people would phone or write to Kalusha with malicious allegations against me. Bitterly disappointed men who realised I was now out of their reach, my former boss at the TV station, women admirers who wanted Kalusha for themselves. The list of people bent on destroying the marriage was big. It also included close family members!

Our baby was due in a few months. Kalusha's parents suggested it was best for me to stay with them in Zambia so that I would get better care and support. Being young and inexperienced, I was going to need help with the baby. I flew back to Zambia to live with my aunt on the Copperbelt, instead. That's what my parents preferred.

Two months before the baby was born, rumours started making the rounds that I had given birth to a 'coloured Indian' baby. In no time the rumour spread like wildfire. They said that I had been unfaithful to Kalusha and was now paying the price. "She has given birth to another man's child and Kalusha's decided to end the marriage."

Those who despised me, including some stepsisters, loved this. They spread the lies even more. In no time, the whole country was talking about the shameful Maureen who cheated on her man. Some swore that they had seen the coloured baby. Very few people knew that I was still heavily pregnant and safely hidden away in a nice quiet place. Kalusha also heard the rumour. He phoned to urge me to stay calm for the sake of the baby's health. But the lies spread out of control. Some said I had an affair with an Indian man who owned a shop in town. In fact, the Indian man they talked

52

about was a former class mate and having an affair was the last thing on both our minds. Others said I had a child with a certain Asian TV sports presenter. This was very hurtful to both him and me. He was a respectable conservative Muslim who would not even shake the hand of a woman. The only time I spoke to him was to greet him when he came to the TV studios to present his show. Almost every man I was seen with, was said to have had an affair with me, and the list was long. My detractors were bent on causing as much damage to my reputation as possible. It didn't matter who they hurt in the process. They just wanted Kalusha and me to split at all cost.

Newspaper editors requested to take photographs of me to prove that I was still pregnant. My father refused. He would not play along to the malice of foolish people, he said. In hindsight, I wish the photos had been taken and published. It would have stopped the lies.

When I went into labour, I had to take a one hour drive from Ndola to Luanshya, where I was booked to deliver the baby at the mine hospital. Staff on duty waited outside the ward to see what kind of baby would be born. Word spread that Maureen Nkandu was in labour. Mobs of people camped outside the hospital, eagerly waiting to hear if indeed the baby was 'coloured'. Police were called in to ensure my safety. After eight hours in labour, I gave birth to a baby girl. She was slightly underweight but in good health. The midwife gasped. "Oh my God! This child looks exactly like Kalusha. She's a spitting image of him, even at this early stage. Why would people be so malicious", she wanted to know, wiping tears off her face.

I was exhausted and delighted the baby had come. Kalusha phoned me at the hospital to say "Congratulations. I'll get time from work to come and see you and the baby. Get some rest now". I fell asleep.

Two weeks later, he flew in to see the baby. He cuddled the child and burst into tears. He said he had to rush back because he had a crucial game to play soon. He told me that he would be back to take me and baby girl along. The infant had to be at least a month old before she could take the ten hour flight to Europe. I did not hear from him again. He ignored my calls and didn't respond to my letters. Next, his uncle informed my parents that he had decided to end the marriage. He didn't say why.

The mood at home was sombre. My mother and father wept. Kalusha's parents travelled to Lusaka to meet my parents and try to find a solution. They too wept. I was in a state of shock. Why would Kalusha end it between us without a word? He promised to come back to fetch me and the baby. Did he believe the lies? Did he not see that the child looked like him? I wondered why life was so unfair. I had never cheated on him. Why and where did the rumour of the coloured baby start from? Was it because my family was dysfunctional and an embarrassment? I had a lot of questions. I cried myself to sleep every night. Meanwhile, my sisters, workmates at ZNBC, including the pesky boss and others celebrated openly. They had won.

Kalusha and I did not communicate again. I wrote letters to him. He didn't reply. I became the centre of public ridicule. I was humiliated. They said that I brought shame to myself and my family. They called me a bitch, a gold digger who had slept around with men, mainly Indians, for their money. The only Indians I knew were my former school mates. How and why was I to ignore them when I met them in public? They were my friends and I had to be free to chat and associate with them. My father said the people who started the rumour knew very well what they were doing. He even said he knew who they were. He mentioned my former boss at ZNBC, who had repeatedly harassed me for sexual favours, as one of the main culprits. He was spiteful because I never gave in to him, whereas he had affairs with almost every other girl at ZNBC. Girls fought and fell over themselves to date him. It hurt when people said that I was his girlfriend, but that's the impression he created.

I became reclusive. I could not go anywhere without people pointing fingers at me. When I stepped out with the child, people would take a peep just to check the race of the baby. I had no job, was stuck at home with a child whose father did not want us. The pain of losing my first ever love, a man who had promised to protect and never hurt me, was too much. I went into depression and lost a lot of weight.

After months of sitting in my room crying, my father told me to keep my chin up. "You need to move on. He clearly doesn't want you. One day the truth will be known," he said. "He has physical talent, you have intellectual talent. His will die, yours will live on beyond you. Get up and be Maureen again," he urged me.

With these words, I woke up the following morning, polished myself and went to ask for my job back at ZNBC. There was no debate about it. They wanted me back. The following week, I was on TV reading news. The nation went ecstatic. The switchboard phone did not stop ringing. There were hundreds of messages of good will. I realised that not the whole world was against me after all.

A year later, in 1989 I heard through a newspaper article that Kalusha got married. Although I was hurt, for I had always hoped we would get back together, I moved on with my life. I admitted again that the annoying Tanzanian prophet was right when he told me that I would not marry Kalusha. Kalusha and I never spoke or wrote to each other. He sent support for the child through his family. I also got tremendous support from Catholic Priest, Father Charles Chilinda, who was a student Jesuit priest then. He and a Polish priest called Henry Prill, literally lifted me out of my pain and desolation. They checked on me and the baby almost every day and made sure that we had what we needed. They were God-sent.

Dating Again

I had managed to pull myself together after my very public break up. The ridicule and finger-pointing continued but it didn't bother me. I walked with my head up. I felt that as long as those who mattered knew the truth, the rest could go to hell. They were of no consequence to my life.

I went to college abroad, to the Indian Institute of Mass Communications to study for a Diploma in Journalism. I also had specialised training in all aspects of television. My confidence was also buoyed by my having won broadcasting awards in 1989 and 1990 as the best Television Newsreader in Zambia.

The following year, former Iraqi president, Saddam Hussein's regime annexed Kuwait. It was a global news story and war between the West and Iraq was imminent. Then US president, George Bush and the United Nations urged Saddam to withdraw from Kuwait or face a forceful attack. Iraq believed that historically Kuwait belonged to them.

I liked international affairs and was sometimes assigned stories on global developments. In this case, I was asked to produce a current affairs package on the Iraqi crisis. This was my first break at analytical reporting and I was determined to do it well. I contacted the representatives of the belligerent parties for their perspectives. The US Embassy in Lusaka provided a written statement from the State Department - the equivalent of the foreign ministry.

The Iraqi ambassador was keen on giving his views. But he first had to get clearance from his government. Zambia and Iraq had excellent diplomatic relations and the leaders of the two countries were good friends. President Kaunda and Saddam Hussein even shared the same birth date - April 27. Next day, I recorded an interview with the ambassador of Iraq. I also taped comments from Kuwaiti officials, others in the gulf region, the Zambian government and of course the statement from the U.S. Embassy.

The TV report was well received, mainly by the Iraqis. They requested a copy of the tape to share with the administration in Baghdad. The ambassador invited me to dinner. The invitation came through the representative of one of the diplomatic missions in Lusaka, the Palestine Liberation Organisation (PLO) in Zambia, who was a good friend of the media. He often hosted parties at his house for journalists. Some were suspicious and suggested that his social events were a pretext for getting unofficial information from journalists. But he was a pleasant and well liked man.

An upmarket conservative restaurant was chosen. I booked a taxi from home and showed up on time, but found that a few other invited guests were already seated. They all stood up to greet me. The PLO representative did the introductions: there was an official attached to the Ministry of Finance by the Egyptian government; two security officials from the Syrian government of former President Hafez Al Assad of Syria; a Lebanese billionaire based in Paris and, of course, the Iraqi ambassador.

Dinner was great. We discussed Middle East politics as well as Zambian issues. For me this was a first-hand lesson in the Gulf conflict, albeit from a skewed perspective. The men also shared a lot of jokes. I felt like a diamond among rough rocks. I enjoyed being surrounded by these powerful men. We finished in the early hours.

The following day I went back to work well informed about what was happening in the Gulf region. I also had a roaring, passionate affair with one of the men at the dinner table, albeit a long-distance relationship, for months to come. My mother knew about the affair and was happy when my lover approached her for my hand in marriage so that he could whisk my daughter and me away to his country in the Middle East. I wasn't ready. My public break-up still haunted me and I was afraid of commitment. Long distance relationships hardly ever work so ours died a natural death.

Then came a Rather Peculiar Proposal...

Months after the Iraq- Kuwait war, I got a message after I finished reading news on TV that a man named Mr Chileshe Chileshe (not his real name) had phoned wanting to speak to me urgently. The only Mr Chileshe I knew was my aunt's husband on the Copperbelt. He fought often with his wife and she would run away to stay with other family members. She had not come by this time so I wondered why my uncle wanted to speak to me. He never called me at work.

I was used to receiving phone calls on the studio line. Apart from the usual fans and suitors, I also got calls from family and friends. The switchboard number was the only way of getting hold of me when I was at work. I didn't have an office or a personal phone line and we had no mobile phones back then. The operator would patch my calls to the engineer's control room next to the studio. The technicians complained that the persistent phone calls for me blocked other important in coming calls, registering a technical fault or a transmission black out. These cases required urgent attention, such as guidance or an announcement or apology to viewers. Besides, the director general or chief engineer of ZNBC would also phone to check if all was okay. Often the line was engaged because I was speaking to a fan or family member. I got the reputation for congesting the phone line. "We are not your personal assistants so stop telling people to phone you here," one of my workmates shouted at me angrily.

But on the night that Mr Chileshe phoned, I was told to make haste and answer his call. It was from State House. Anyone associated with State House was given prime importance. It is the office of the head of state and carries the highest authority in the land. People would drop what they were doing to rush there if they were summoned, even by the most junior officer.

Mr Chileshe introduced himself as a man working in the Office of the President. He said that someone very senior in government had instructed him to discuss an important matter with me and he wanted to meet me the following day. He would pick me up from work and take me to a quiet place where we would discuss a marriage proposal. I was not to tell anybody about our meeting or the conversation. I was instructed to tell the technicians who'd taken Mr Chileshe's call that he was a long-lost uncle. Period.

The next day, the emissary picked me up in an old VW Beetle. We drove to a quiet place where he parked his car. He went straight to the point. "His Excellency has asked me to get in touch with you with a very serious proposal. He has a nephew who is interested in you and would like to marry you. His Excellency thinks that you would be suitable for his nephew. He is keen on this marriage happening very soon. He knows your parents, he has known you since you were a baby and he likes you a lot. So what do you say?"

I didn't know what to say. I had never had such a proposal before. A lot of things swiftly ran through my mind. Why would the president get personally involved in this matter? I was quiet for a moment. "I will think about it and get back to you," I responded. Mr Chileshe told me that I had to do so quickly because the president considered this matter urgent.

The following evening after my shift, Mr Chileshe phoned to find out if I had made up my mind. There was a great sense of urgency around him. I was nervous and confused. I didn't know whether to speak to anyone about this proposal. He had instructed me to keep this matter confidential until all the basic issues had been concluded. But I didn't trust him. I pondered on a lot of issues. Who was the man interested in marrying me and why didn't he ask me himself?

At our second meeting, Mr Chileshe was accompanied by another gentleman whom he said was a workmate. They gave me the details of the man who wanted to be my hubby. His name sounded like it was from the Northern Province. I cannot remember it because I was completely disinterested.

I was told that he hailed from Isoka. They also told me that he was a strong member of the ruling United National Independence Party (UNIP) Youth Wing and that his hostel dormitory had recently been torched by irate students who were protesting poor conditions at the campus and general price increases in the country. "They accused him of being an informer. He survived by the Grace of God," they said. Then it clicked; they were taking me for a ride. The president was from Chinsali not Isoka, so how was my suitor his nephew? Maybe from his mother's side? I didn't know what to think.

Although the whole arrangement seemed odd, I was eager to meet this man. It was arranged that he travel from his hideout for the purpose. I was picked up from work around 6 p.m. by Mr Chileshe and driven to a dingy restaurant in Woodlands. When we entered the secluded room, I saw three men already seated, waiting. I quickly assessed them. None of them looked like the kind I would want to be married to. "Perhaps this so-called husband of mine will come in later," I thought. I imagined that if he was the president's nephew, he must probably be affluent and worthy of my time.

When I sat down, I was pleased to learn that he was none of the three gentlemen. I breathed a sigh of relief. Then he stepped in. He could barely walk. He limped towards us. He was dark, of medium height, slim and not good looking at all. I was disappointed. I didn't like the way he was dressed either. He leaned forward to hug me, but I stretched out my hand to greet him. Others in the room watched keenly. He remarked at how much prettier I looked in person than on TV. He was not my type. "Yuck," I thought.

They offered me a drink. I declined. Then my 'suitor' introduced himself. He gave a long list of his political activities as a youth leader. He explained that some students were jealous of him because of his political connections. That is why they tried to kill him. They accused him of being a government informer. He explained that his foot was badly injured when he tried to escape his burning college room.

I didn't know whether to laugh or cry. I hated the way he looked, the way he spoke, the things he said. "What makes this man think that I would marry him?" I thought. I was angry, disgusted and wanted to go home. I thanked the gentlemen for the proposal and said that I would get back to them. They dropped me off at my shared apartment in the evening.

I couldn't sleep that night. A lot of thoughts went through my mind. I wondered what kind of marriage proposal this was. According to what I knew someone from my family ought to have been there when the proposal was being discussed. And why didn't he speak to me himself? Why was the president's name included in this whole messy thing? How was I to marry a stranger, someone I met only that night? Did they expect me to fall in love with him instantly? Why did the discussion have to remain secret? And why did they tape record the conversations?

I was sure that Mr Chileshe was making a recording because he'd opened his briefcase at the beginning of the meeting, touched something in it, and then appeared to switch off something soon after that, before closing the briefcase. And why did they ask me a lot of questions about my family, especially my father? That's it… I sat up in my bed. The marriage proposal was fake. I suspected they wanted to get to my father. But why and for what?

Mr Chileshe was persistent. He called me in the morning saying my husband-to-be would be travelling to Isoka to meet the chief and wanted to go there with good news about the marriage. I was determined to tell him it wouldn't work. I wasn't interested. But before I could answer, he quickly interjected and suggested another meeting that evening at the same restaurant in Woodlands.

There were very few people in the restaurant. This time Mr Chileshe showed up with two other men, both wearing dark tinted glasses. There was an ominous look about them. Maybe they had sensed that I wasn't interested in their proposal because I knew their true motive. But what was their motive? To get information about my dad? To dupe me into some marriage…. to kill me… maybe they were enemies of my dad. Or my enemies! But why? I hadn't done anything wrong. Neither had my father, as far as I was concerned. I had heard stories about how people in other countries disappeared. So who really were Mr Chileshe and his lackeys and why me? I was alone with strange men in a quiet, drab restaurant. What if they drove me away to kill me? If they took me away, no one would ever know what had happened. I was afraid. I wished I had informed my parents about this whole thing.

Again, Mr Chileshe opened his briefcase. This time I was sure that I saw the small tape recorder. He asked me what my stand was regarding the marriage. "I have thought about it and think that it won't be possible because I don't know the man well. I can't get married to a stranger," I told the three men.

62

"That's well understood," said Mr Chileshe. "We will give you time to know him. Eventually you'll spend more time with him and I am sure you'll fall in love." The two other men hardly spoke. They gave me strange looks which made me very nervous and unsettled.

They offered me a lift home after the meeting. As soon as they dropped me off, I ran down the road, flagged down a taxi and rushed to my parents' house. It was after 10 p.m. by the time I got there. They were pleased that I came in to tell them what happened although my mother angrily chided that I ought to have mentioned this earlier. My father said to leave it with him. He would deal with the matter.

I never heard from Mr Chileshe, my suitor or the other ominous-looking men again. To this day, I have not been able to figure out what it is exactly Mr Chileshe wanted from me.

Why I left ZNBC and Zambia

Although I enjoyed my fortune and fame at ZNBC, my troubles started the day I joined the organisation. I suffered one proposal after another from my supervisor and other men. Many of them fell by the wayside, but my boss was unrelenting. For years he threatened to sack me if I refused to go out with him. He'd give it a break for a few weeks then get back to his proposals. He even whispered to his friends that I was 'his girl'. I despised him. I loved broadcasting and had no other place to go as we had only one TV station in the country at that time.

One day, when I was still dating Kalusha, I met my boss at a party. I had gone there with my friends. He walked up to me, grasped my hand and insisted on walking around the place with me, hands clutched, so that people could see that I was cheating on Kalu.

On another night, he showed up at my flat just before midnight. He said he had been having drinks in the area, was intoxicated and couldn't drive so asked to sleep on my couch. I told him it would look very bad if he slept at my house because we'd be suspected of having an affair. He promised he'd get up very early as soon as he'd sobered up, and leave. He didn't. Then the office land cruiser rocked up at 6:15 a.m. to pick me up, packed with workmates! My boss's car was parked outside my flat. It was a well calculated plan. He knew that I'd be picked up early in the morning and wanted to create a rumour about us. That is how desperate he was. The look on the faces of the people in the car that morning could have killed me. He came out of the house and gleefully walked to his car, whistling as the people in the ZNBC vehicle watched in amazement. I didn't say a word. I couldn't even greet them. The shame was too much. I just wanted to find a quiet corner and cry.

His girlfriend harassed me for months. She threatened to beat me up. She mobilised other women at the TV station against me. They called me all sorts of names. But I had had nothing to do with her idiotic man. The harassment became too much; him running after me, and his girlfriend threatening to deface and bewitch me. I couldn't report him to anyone because he'd created the impression I was his girlfriend and they wouldn't believe me. Besides, who was I to report him to? I didn't trust his superiors.

When I turned him down for the umpteenth time, he removed me from the news desk and sent me to the commercial department to work as a marketing officer. I refused to work there. Fortunately, in early 1992 I got sponsorship from the Norwegian Development Agency (NORAD) for a TV course at the Radio Netherlands Training Centre in Hilversum, Holland. I had six months of peace and focus. But my being away didn't deter his resolve. As soon as I got back, he started his proposals again. Invitations to dinner, to night clubs, offers of gifts such as perfume, which I turned down. He decided to set my colleagues against me. I was in trouble and dreaded going to work.

My other challenge came from other female broadcasters at the TV station. Some of them loathed me! They hated the public attention and huge fan base I was drawing. They ran stories about me that made my life unbearable. They tried to undermine me. It brought back painful parallels with the hell I was going through at home with my stepsisters. "Why do people hate me so much?" I asked my father. "It is because you are good at what you do. You draw a lot of public attention. If you were useless, no one would care about you," he replied.

Back to my woes at ZNBC. Weeks later a senior government official at the Ministry of Information called me to his office to say that they'd decided to transfer me to the Zambia Information Services - ZIS, now called ZANIS. What was I to do there? I was a broadcaster. Was this a plot to destroy my career and if so why? I was later to learn that the ministry official was having an affair with a female presenter at ZNBC, who wanted me out of the way for her own fame. People had destroyed my marriage, my reputation and now wanted to destroy my career. That was the last straw. I refused to move to ZIS and instead decided to leave ZNBC.

Fortunately, towards the end of 1992 BOP Television in the former homeland of Bophuthatswana, South Africa, headhunted me for a lead role as TV presenter. The offer couldn't have come at a better time. At ZNBC, I'd been taken off the news desk and I was not assigned to reporting duty. I'd show up at work and sit in the office the whole day then go back home sad and frustrated.

A few days before I left ZNBC, the assignment editor decided to schedule me for news reading. My boss phoned to yell at him. He was warned never to put me in front of the camera or he'd lose his job. Some colleagues knew that I was being persecuted for not succumbing to his demands. They sympathised with me but there was nothing they could do to help.

My domestic situation didn't help much either. I was scorned and ridiculed by my family. Life at home was unbearable. My mother was hardly ever there. She travelled a lot to Botswana for business. In a way, I felt for her. She had been married off at an early age against her will, then married my father years later and spent her life looking after her children, his children and hordes of other relatives. Her escape was always to leave town. She needed respite. The story is that she always wanted to get a good education through the Catholic mission schools and her parents knew this. She grew up in Kalomo, in the Southern Province, where her family settled after they left Lundazi. One morning when she was fourteen years old her father collected her from class with her bags packed from home. She was elated, thinking she was going to a mission school. But my grandfather had other plans. He had already collected *lobola* (bride price) from a young man and she instead was handed to him in marriage. My poor mother was stuck. After four children, she decided she'd had enough, so she ran away to join her mother, now divorced and living in Kabwe. While there, my mother joined the welfare society, known colloquially as *Olofeya*. She was too old to go back to school so she turned to learning home economics and other skills such as needlework, cookery, arts and crafts.

A few years later, in 1966 she met my father. I was born the following year. My mother was always warm, cheerful and full of life, but my public break-up humiliated her and changed her forever. She told me that what happened to me made her stop believing in the goodness of mankind. She was hurt inside and I could see her cry, secretly. Going away from home was perhaps one way of dealing with the pain of my public humiliation and other issues. But I resented her for not being around, especially for my little girl, Tamela, who absolutely adored her grandmother.

With all this mess, I thought leaving Zambia would be good. At least I'd be too far away to be a constant reminder of the trials my family was going through because of my bruised public image. I didn't know whether to blame it on myself, other people, or my family. One thing for sure is that my family changed. I hated myself and wished that I had not been born.

I was also disappointed by the fact that my father, who was among the thirteen who met at Garden House in Lusaka West in early 1990, as a public defiance of Dr Kaunda's one party state, was completely side-lined and ignored by Frederick Chiluba's government when the country turned to multiparty politics in 1991. There had been underground talks on plural politics. They sometimes met in our house. 'The Garden House 13', as they were called offered Zambians a true glimpse of the brave faces that dared to defy the one-party rule.

My father's being ignored by Chiluba's government after 1991 brought back painful childhood memories of how we suffered when we returned from Nairobi; my mother's constant complaints about Dr Kaunda side-lining Dad for political appointments year after year, despite his overt and powerful contribution to the liberation struggle. He was also talented, educated and would have served his country well. Now decades later, my workmates laughed at me. They made fun of how my dad did so much against UNIP only to be ignored by 'his fellow Bemba man'.

Dad said he was side-lined because he was not an immoral and corrupt person. "If I was, I would have grovelled and stooped low for a job. I am a man of integrity and I have principles. I'd rather eat the leaves that fall off a tree than be associated with what is turning out to be a den of thieves!" he said. He also made me promise that I'd never beg for a government job. "Use your intellect to achieve your goals and no other means," was my father's advice.

My professional and personal challenges were mounting; pressure and resentment at work; instability and confusion at home; my father slumping into reclusion and semi-depression, my reputation severely dented by stupid malicious lies; a single mother with a young child! It was too much for me. All these negative factors made it very easy for me to leave the country. After all I had a good job and an opportunity to start afresh elsewhere. So, at the end of 1992 I packed my bags, took my daughter and left for South Africa. I wondered whether I'd ever come back home.

The Glitz and Glamour of BOP TV

Settling down in Mmabatho, Bophuthatswana, now called the NorthWest Province of South Africa was quite alright. I was accommodated in a modern and fully-furnished company townhouse. I walked straight into a life of comfort. I was also assisted to settle in by comrades and very good friends from the African National Congress, who had been in exile in Zambia years before. Some of them had worked for Radio Freedom, stationed at ZNBC. The channel would broadcast information externally, on the fight against the racist government in South Africa, key messages from leaders in exile like the late Oliver Tambo, as well as those in prison including the late Nelson Mandela and Walter Sisulu. The channel also countered daily propaganda churned out by the apartheid regime's Radio RSA, which was transmitted outside the country. When the ANC and other black liberation movements were unbanned in 1990, many exiles decided to return home. I was delighted to be among them, to experience the resettling and to follow the contentious political situation.

Apartheid was still rife and strong when I went to South Africa and homelands or Bantustans such as Bophuthatswana, Transkei, Ciskei, etc., served as stooge regimes for the racist government. The ANC was banned in BOP, and some of my comrades were not too pleased that I'd decided to work for a TV station there. Others encouraged me to stay, saying things were due to change in the country and it would be good for me to be positioned there already. They thought I'd be a good conduit on information of what was going on around the government of Lucas Mangope, leader of the homeland.

BOP TV was quite an experience. I was quickly groomed into a glamorous front line presenter. I had a free wardrobe sponsored by a top designer *Sacha and Bianca*; I had free make-up and other perks, which made my job a pleasure. I co-anchored a weekly magazine programme titled *Panorama*, with renowned media personality, the late Aubrey Harris. We travelled around the country to produce insets for the show and interviewed famous and infamous people. It was a non-political show. I am certain the M-Net's Carte Blanch programme was modelled around *Panorama*.

However, it was not all rosy when I started work. The style of presentation I was accustomed to in Zambia didn't work at BOP TV. They said I was newsy, dull and boring. I had to liven up and bring out my personality more. It was hard at first. I was a hard-wired newsreader. But after a few months, I got the gist of it and was enjoying my programme. There was also the petty jealousy. Some locals couldn't understand why I was brought all the way from Zambia to present the country's most watched TV show. They tried to sabotage my work and to frustrate me. This was not new. I had been through the same at ZNBC so I was up to the challenge. I loved TV cameras and everything that went with a studio. I always found comfort in being in the studio. Just like at ZNBC, it was the one place where the crowd was shut out, and I was in control. Nobody could stop me from shining when I was on camera. That is when I was at my happiest. I also felt the same years later when I worked for the BBC in London.

I travelled a lot and worked at night sometimes. Child care for my little daughter was hard. We didn't have family or close friends to help. I depended on the goodwill of my acquaintances to babysit for me when I was out of town or working during weekends. My daughter's nanny didn't live in and she didn't work weekends. I sometimes found it difficult to focus or concentrate on my job because I worried about whether she had been picked up from school, if she had eaten or whether she was safe. I missed my family in Zambia despite some of them having been horrible to me. I also wished that my mother could come and live with me and help me with the child, but she said she was busy with her business. I eventually discovered a few Zambians in the town. They were very kind and helped with my little girl.

The radio and TV station was run by young, talented, dynamic broadcasters and journalists. More than 80 percent of us were under twenty five years old. We were nationals from various African countries, the Middle East and Europe – a mini United Nations.

The regime of Lucas Mangope was repressive and there was no freedom of expression. They kept a close eye on me because of my known links with ANC comrades. In late November 1993, I was visited by an ANC operative whom I had met during his *Umkhonto we Sizwe* days in exile in Zambia. He sneaked into Mmabatho driving a VW Golf with a fake Bophuthatswana number plate. It would have been harder to detect him as an outsider than if he had the recognisable Transvaal number plate. We chatted about my work, life in Mangopeland and the political situation in Zambia. I argued strongly against his allegation that former President Chiluba was corrupt. Despite his side-lining my father, Chiluba was a hero for his part in unseating Kenneth Kaunda. As far as I was concerned the latter was more responsible for wasting my father's political talent and ambition than Chiluba was.

My friend said that he and other South African trade unionists had interacted with Mr Chiluba and were more aware of his corrupt nature than most Zambians. He also tipped me that KK would be visiting BOP soon at the request of the ANC to hold talks with President Lucas Mangope. As our heated discussion went on, I heard footsteps outside. They were very soft but I could pick them up. I got up quietly to peep through the window and saw two figures quickly walking away from my house. I realised that they had been outside all along, eavesdropping on our conversation. No doubt they had picked up that my guest didn't belong to the city and were curious to know who he was. That's how the regime operated. Mangope, supported by the apartheid regime, and possibly by the Israelis, too, had an astute and brutal intelligence network.

Sensing danger, my friend decided to leave as soon as he felt it safe, that same night. He was sure they'd come back for him and he didn't want to compromise my career and security. He scribbled instructions on a piece of paper. At the bottom it read: *"Tear this to pieces ASAP and burn in the grill with a piece of steak."* They'd think I was grilling meat and not destroying important information. Around 10 p.m. he jumped over my backyard wall, walked on foot to the taxi rank and got the last minibus leaving for a remote town, from where he was to take another minibus to Johannesburg the following morning. I was to tell others that my 'boyfriend' had brought me a small car to use because I had none. The following weekend I was to drive it to the shops and leave it unlocked, with the plan of finding it 'stolen' when I got back from the shops. This theft was not to be reported. The car had to leave Mmabatho as quickly as possible otherwise they'd have traced where it came from and find out that it had a fake number plate. That, too, would have put me in trouble. Even though I was rid of my friend and the car, I felt vulnerable. His written message on the piece of paper was very clear. *"Get out of here as soon as you can. There is trouble coming!"*

I was troubled. Where could I go? I had a young child and going back to Zambia almost a year after I'd left was not an option. I could not bear the thought of returning to ZNBC. My family had disintegrated. My mother had left my dad and my siblings were all over the place. There was no home to go to. I had to think very fast. As God would have it, I got a letter from Radio Netherlands Training Centre in Hilversum, where I'd trained in TV the year before, offering me a scholarship to study all aspects of radio. They were to pay for my air ticket, accommodation, and living expenses for the six month course! I knelt and thanked God profoundly. The only catch was that I couldn't take my child with me. What was I to do? I had to leave Mmabatho. I sensed that my colleagues' and even my boss' attitude towards me had changed. My boss was the favourite daughter of Lucas Mangope. Although she and I were good friends, I was sure that her father's interest came first. I was smart enough to know that they didn't trust me and it was a matter of time before they'd pick me up for questioning. I'd heard horror stories of how people were locked up, tortured or disappeared on the slightest suspicion of collaborating or befriending anyone from the ANC. I was not going to pass the chance of going to Holland to study and I was just as determined to leave. My plan was that I'd use the time I was in Europe to think of my next destination, possibly within Europe, where I'd settle with my daughter after I'd finished my studies and found a job. Foolhardy perhaps, but I had the faith. Then a distant cousin in Lusaka offered to take care of my daughter.

At the end of November, I gave a month's notice to resign from BOP TV. I cited my reason as wanting to pursue further studies in Europe. My resignation was reluctantly accepted. Late December, I took my daughter to Zambia. It was one of the most heart-breaking experiences of my life. I loved her very much, spent every day with her and now had to be separated from her for six months. She was five years old and needed to be with her mother. I was going to miss playing with her, reading her stories, doing her hair and singing songs to her every night. She'd sleep in my bed and we'd clutch hands very tightly, a mark of bonding and closeness. How was my little girl going to cope without me? This was not the first time I'd separated from her. When she was two years old, I left her with my parents while I studied for my Diploma in Journalism in India. She cried for me every day, as I did for her. I swore never to be separated from her again. She was a very special child. I remember crying all the way to Zambia and on my flight to Holland a few days later. I hated and blamed myself for everything that was happening to me. But very painful memories of life in Zambia made me even more determined to go as far away as possible from the place.

Almost two months after my daughter and I had left Mmabatho, in February 1994, the place was on fire. Violence broke out as pro-ANC troops marched into the town and took over. They were wildly cheered and supported by the local people. The regime of Lucas Mangope collapsed. There was a massive uprising, rioting, looting and it was dangerous to be there, especially for foreigners, whom incoming troops and even the people of Mmabatho considered traitors and collaborators with the Mangope and apartheid regimes. Mangope's soldiers offered very little resistance. His support came from racist white troops from nearby towns, some of whom were summarily executed in full view of global TV cameras. Bophuthatswana was no more. I phoned my ANC comrade to thank him for the timely warning to get out! I got on my knees and praised God.

After BOP TV ... Life in Europe

I was now safe and snug in Holland. My course was intense but rewarding. I spent every evening in the computer room, looking for a job. The course was six months and I needed somewhere to go after that. My father insisted that I return home. But he was feeble, jobless and abandoned by his wife and other children. How was I to return to a place like that? Just before the course ended, I was offered a freelance role at the Radio Netherlands International. It didn't pay much but it was enough for Tamela and me to live on. Beyond the part-time job, I also enrolled to study for a master's degree in journalism at the University of Wales. The course was starting the following year in 1995. Using the second sector of my return ticket bought for me by the training centre, I returned to Zambia in June 1994, expressly to collect my daughter. I had no plan of staying.

When I went back to Zambia to fetch my Tamela, I had no money for our air tickets back to Europe. Armed with confidence and enthusiasm, I phoned an old friend, the late former finance minister, Mr Ronald Penza, to ask for two one-way tickets to Amsterdam, where I was to be based while waiting to commence my MA studies the following year. It was July 1994 and I was twenty-seven years old. Mr Penza called a friend at a travel agency to give me the tickets on account that I'd pay back. I had no means of doing so in the foreseeable future but was sure that I could pay back one day. I was bold, stubborn, foolish but ambitious. I had strong faith and always set out to achieve what others deemed impossible. I knew that my faith, plus my looks, always got me what I wanted. The following day, my daughter and I were in Johannesburg en route to Amsterdam! We were to stay with a friend until we were ready to fend for ourselves. I still had my part-time radio job and had made some applications for sponsorship for my studies.

My parents were not pleased that I did not heed their advice to leave the child with either of them. "How will you study with a young child in a foreign land?" my mother cried. But I was determined to go with her. The thought of being away from my little girl even for another day, was unimaginable. Besides, the family was not together anymore, it had disintegrated and I didn't trust anyone. I hated home.

Tamela and I had several hours to pass at the airport in Johannesburg before our flight to Holland. We had arrived from Lusaka on the afternoon flight and were only due to connect to Amsterdam in the evening. Although we knew a few people in Johannesburg, we decided to stay at the airport. Besides, it was a weekday and people might be too busy to fetch us and bring us back in time for the evening flight. We didn't want to be a bother.

Tamela was also hungry and wanted something to eat. I had very little money on me - only enough to see us through one month until I got paid for my freelance work. So I bought her a few snacks from the airport store to keep her happy. Tamela was a contented little girl, disciplined and often did as she was told. She was ecstatic that she was going to live in Europe with her mother.

As we paced about the airport departure lounge, we were greeted by a young man dressed in a South Africa Airways uniform. He said he was from Zambia and recognised me from television. He was very kind and friendly and gave me his business card. His name was Daniel Mundea. He invited us for a drink at the airport restaurant but I turned down his offer. We had had enough for the day and just wanted to fly out.

"Who's that mommy?" asked Tamela. "Oh just someone who says he knows me from TV," I said. We had a pleasant flight to Amsterdam and for the next few months enjoyed the hospitality of Irene and her family.

The MA course was intense. I was to study in three European cities as part of my thesis research on The Image of Africa in Western Media. The BBC was my main case study, but I also had subjects in EU integration and international relations so I had to move around. The degree course was designed in such a way that we'd spend the first leg at Utrecht University in Holland, then Arhus School of Journalism in Denmark and finally, University of Wales in Cardiff, where I was to finalise and submit my thesis. Some people thought I was crazy to do this with a young child. I thought they lacked ambition and courage.

A few weeks later I was surprised to receive a letter from Daniel. I hadn't given him my address so how did he know where to find me? All I had told him was that I was going to study and work part-time at Radio Netherlands. Years later I discovered that he had searched around for the address of the radio station. They had my forwarding address, so his mail finally reached me. I had forgotten all about him. I read the top line of his letter and tossed it away. It wasn't interesting. I had always received lots of fan mail and I didn't find this one any different. Dozens of fans talked about how they admired me, or might name their daughters after me, etc.; I was tired of their pleasantries.

The university's accounts department told me that they wanted a letter of guarantee from my bank, or sponsors, that my fees would be paid in full. I had been offered a place on the premise that I would get sponsors for the one year degree course, but almost a month into my studies I had not made any payments. I had to produce the letter or risk being kicked out. The thought of going back to Zambia, to that dysfunctional family terrified me. I still had no money or any idea where I was going to get it from. But as always, I had faith in God. I believed a funder would come up soon.

When I was at BOP TV I had heard of a South African tycoon businessman called Koos Bekker, who had set up the private pay TV channel M-Net. They said he was based in Holland, heading the Nethold Group of companies, which included a private TV station. I looked for his contacts and made an appointment to see him. Armed with charm, confidence and brilliance, I walked into his office and got straight to the point. I was a Zambian student eager to learn, but with no money and needed sponsorship. After interviewing me for about fifteen minutes, he said he'd think about it but I should go back, put my request in writing and mail it to him. I asked him for a piece of paper and pen, drafted my letter of request, signed and handed it to him there and then. He smiled and said, "Yes, we will sponsor your studies. Give my assistant your bank details."

Months into my stay in Holland, I befriended a senior radio journalist at Radio Netherlands, where I had done some freelance work previously. We became very good friends. I confided in him about my family problems and how much I didn't want to go back to Zambia. We became intimate and he provided for me like a lover would. He continued to support me after I returned to Holland with Tamela. But one day he decided to cut me off. We had had a few misunderstandings. He was married. I wanted more of him. Realistically this was not possible. But I was used to getting what I wanted. My sulking and being grumpy got the better of him. So he left.

He never called me or came to see me. I was on my own. I moved on very quickly.

With the sponsorship funds from Nethold Group, I moved out of Irene's house to rent a room in a lovely big house close to the school my daughter attended. We lived on my student allowance. It was very small and I only had enough money to buy food, pay the rent and cover transport costs. I had no choice but to ask Kalusha to help me with child support. He did, whenever he could and I'd use it to buy my daughter clothes and other needs. Kalusha and I only spoke on the phone and never saw each other. He lived in another town with his family. It was very clear that we were both done and dusted, although I sometimes missed him. I'd smile to myself each time I remembered his jokes. Then the pain would hit me and I'd cry.

It was tough to be away from family, in a foreign cold land, but what was I to do? By now I had become accustomed to crying. I cried every night after I'd put my Tamela to bed. I lost a lot of weight from my misery but pulled myself together during the day for the sake of my daughter. I didn't want her and others to see that I was unhappy. She was oblivious of our plight. She made friends at school and in the neighbourhood and hardly ever talked about Zambia or South Africa.

Maria, my landlady was pleasant. She lived alone. She became my daughter's godmother and gave her treats. She'd take her and Sean, the neighbour's son, who was Tamela's classmate and best friend, out for picnics, shopping and for fun and games, while I stayed home to do my assignments or study. I cleaned her huge house over the weekend and cooked. We started living like a family rather than landlord and tenant. This was very good for me. I was able to focus on my studies while my daughter felt at home.

The first semester was from January to March 1995. The following month, April, I had to move to Aarhus in Denmark for the second leg of my MA studies which would end in June, before moving to Cardiff in Wales. I had no money for the journey. My sponsors would only send the money later. I explained my situation to Maria and she was sympathetic.

She offered to pay our train fares to Aarhus.

The train journey was via Groningen in the north of Holland, through Munich and Osnabruck in Germany, then on to Copenhagen. From there the train was loaded onto a ferry, and took the onward journey to Aarhus in the north of Denmark. We left Amsterdam around 8 a.m. and arrived in Arhus about 5 p.m. the same day. Both Maria and Tamela had cried bitterly at the parting. So had Sean. The image of Maria holding onto the train and running as it moved off, tears rolling down her face will never leave me. It was another painful moment. The train ride was an exciting and partly scary adventure, especially when we crossed the border into Germany. The sight of police with German shepherd dogs walking through the coaches of the train reminded me of the movies I'd seen of Nazi Germany. I was terrified. Two policemen with a dog came to the coach where Tamela and I were. They spoke only German. I didn't. I told them I was a journalism student on my way to Aarhus in Denmark. I showed them our passports and school letters. One of them gave a nice smile to Tamela. She smiled back. They wished us a good trip and all the best with my studies and moved on to the next coach. I was relieved.

I was glad that my new university professor and other lecturers were impressed by my work. Despite the few challenges, I was sharp, attentive in class, diligent and did my assignments on time. I also got good grades – it was my tradition to. They were amazed at how a young African girl could be so bold as to study in Europe, with a young child. My ambition and determination earned me praise. It also earned me their admiration and support. They arranged for my daughter and me to live free of charge in one of the staff houses on the campus of the Danish School of Journalism. It was a fully furnished four-bedroomed house with all the amenities we needed. I was delighted. Like always, my daughter and I got on our knees and thanked God.

We were happy in Denmark, mostly because we had a nice comfortable home. It was the beginning of spring when we got there so the nice weather cheered us up too. There was only one English-speaking primary school in Arhus, the International School. I couldn't afford the fees so I took Tamela to a nearby Danish one where they had a class of English every week. It was okay. My little girl needed to be in school and to make friends. In no time Tamela could speak perfect Danish. She had already learned Tswana from Mmabatho and Dutch while we were in Holland.

The temptations to fall in love were many. Danish men are generally tall and very good looking and I must admit that I was attracted to some. But I still had open wounds and could not allow myself to fall in love. I was terrified of being dumped again. Besides, I was happy and contented with my new life. Some students at my school thought I was weird. I didn't care. I socialised with my classmates, and had fun whenever I could. I hardly heard from my family, except a letter every two or three weeks from my dad and occasionally one from my brother, Dick who was based in Mozambique. I also received letters from Daniel, the man from South African Airways whom I had met at the airport in Johannesburg months earlier. All he wrote about was funerals, his twin brother and other family members.

Then Cupid's Arrow Hit

My friendship with Daniel grew. We would exchange letters; he phoned me regularly. I was now a friend and he no longer a mere fan. I hardly ever got mail or calls from my family so the few conversations with Daniel kept Tamela and me happy, although at times I found him quite boring. He seemed obsessed by his family. I, on the other hand, was trying hard to get away from mine.

University authorities suggested that for the sake of the child, I stay in Arhus for the final leg of my studies, only traveling to Cardiff to present my thesis and research papers for my graduation. I felt blessed.

One cold day in late October I was stressed, homesick and broke. It was minus thirty-five degrees Celsius outside; the sky was dark in contrast to the inches high white carpet of snow. I couldn't even go out to exchange empty bottles, which I used to pick up from the street when I was broke, and exchange for cash at the local supermarket. I did this often when I ran out of money. I'd even pick empty bottles from the rubbish bins. I had no choice at times. I'd use the money for food and small toys for my daughter. When I got my allowance, I used to send some of it to my father. He was jobless. I'd wrap the money in carbon paper used in typewriters, then insert it in a letter and post it to him. The little I sent helped him get by.

On a very cold wintry day, the house phone rang. I hoped it was my parents or other family members. All I wanted was to hear from them. But it was Daniel on the line. My irritation soon eased when he told me that he had sent me some money. It must have been divine intervention because I had not asked for help from him. When the weather improved Tamela and I dashed out of the house to buy the much-needed groceries.

After I graduated from the University of Wales in Cardiff, I took up a few basic jobs in Arhus and later in Berlin where I worked briefly as head of the International Youth Exchange. I needed to raise money for my and Tamela's tickets to Johannesburg. I was extremely homesick by now and just wanted to go back. I missed the food, the good weather, my friends, my family, including the ill-intentioned ones who had driven me away in the first place.

But what was I to do in Zambia? I didn't want to go back to ZNBC. I hated the politics which had systematically maligned my father for years.

I still had mistrust of the people who had hurt and betrayed me. I decided to go back to South Africa. After all I had friends there, especially in the ANC. It was 1996, the country had held democratic elections and a number of my buddies were in positions of power.

When I'd earned enough for two tickets and a bit extra, it was time to go home. After all, my scholarship from Nethold Group stipulated that I return to South Africa after my studies to work for M-Net. I was excited to return.

In no time, Tamela and I were back in Johannesburg. We rented a backyard flat close to the M-Net studios in Randburg. Management was to decide where to place me and I was asked to wait for a few weeks. I was anxious to start work because I didn't have any money, save for the little that I had saved up from my jobs in Europe.

When I phoned Daniel to tell him that we were back in the country, he offered us accommodation at his house. I was not too comfortable with the idea, but accepted on the understanding that Tamela and I would move out within a month. He had a three-bedroomed house and although two cousins from Zambia were staying with him, there was enough room for my daughter and me. Daniel's cousins were not too pleased with their new guests. I could feel their resentment and hoped that my contract could be issued quickly so that we could move out. They gave me dirty looks. They whispered bad things about me - such as I was stranded in life and now trying to hook their cousin. They also resented the attention Daniel gave me. I didn't find Daniel attractive and I certainly didn't fancy him. I felt that he had an odd outlook on life centred entirely on his family. I was just eager to move out and start my own life.

His house was unkempt. It was often rowdy and crowded, with frequent parties and with people coming in and out. I am a private person so I felt very uneasy. I wished that I hadn't moved in. What choice did I have anyway? It wasn't my house. Mealtimes were uncomfortable. I often cooked supper but hated doing so because I was not the lady of the house. I did it out of politeness and gratitude for the free lodging. It would have been unwise to cook only for my daughter and leave out the others. That's not how I was raised. I remembered my father's wise counsel: "The lack of money will always enslave you."

I moved out of Daniel's place after I settled into my new role as a public relations officer at M-Net. I also featured as guest presenter on the inaugural M-Net broadcast to Africa and later worked as a freelance presenter for the investigative programme, *Carte Blanche*.

Daniel and I continued to see each other. Our conversations became more interesting and fun, especially when they had nothing to do with his family. We shared childhood memories and other stories, dreams, wishes, aspirations. After a long jog one evening, we sat on a bench in a park and watched the sun set. Daniel put his arm around my shoulder and told me that he liked me. He said he had grown fond of me. I was a bit stunned, but it was to be expected. We had been spending a lot of time together and I knew that he found me attractive. So on that beautiful spring evening, Daniel and I kissed in the park.

His cousins were concerned that our relationship would destroy well laid plans for his marriage. He had a fiancée in Zambia and they were due to wed in a few months. He was summoned to Lusaka by his uncles and his bride's family. I suggested to him that we end our relationship. It had happened too quickly and we had to stop it.

But Daniel stunned his relatives. He told them he was breaking the engagement. He wanted me. He jumped on a plane and flew back to Johannesburg. After dating for six months, Daniel proposed to me. I was in love and threw caution to the wind! He suggested I give up my flat and we move back to his house. I did. We spent hours chatting, laughing and taking long romantic walks. We went out to functions, dinner parties, movies and other places. I was now back on TV and living my life to the full. We simply shut out the rest of the world. Although he had a modest job as public relations officer at South Africa Airways we were happy together. We were in total bliss!

His family rejected our marriage plans outright. They said I was wrong for him. I was not the right tribe, and I had come in to break up his planned marriage. He was Lozi and I Bemba. They wanted him to marry a woman from his tribe, or a Tonga. They accused me of being a witch, who had cast a spell on their son.

My family also resented Daniel. They felt that he was from the wrong background, not highly educated and of low social status. But Daniel and I were in love. We defied the advice from our families and decided we would go ahead with our marriage. There was nothing they could do or say to stop us.

Where did I go Wrong

My serious troubles began soon after my engagement to Daniel. There was a lot of pressure on him from his family to end our relationship. I was concerned that the whole thing was tearing his family apart. "How could people be so adamantly against a marriage which was none of their business?" I wondered. Daniel said they were jealous.

They called me names and threatened to disrupt our wedding plans. So I decided to break the engagement. But before I could tell Daniel, I discovered that I was pregnant. He was elated and suggested that we go to Cape Town for a weekend to celebrate. My being with child also meant that we had to hasten our wedding plans. It was April 1997, during the Easter Holiday.

In Cape Town we stayed with Daniel's friend. In the evening when we went out for a meal, I felt tired and wanted to go back home to sleep. I was also unimpressed with Daniel's drinking. I had never seen him drink so much alcohol and it made me uncomfortable in front of our host and other people around us.

Back at his friend's place, Daniel and I had an argument over his drinking. He began to beat me. He punched me in the stomach but mostly on my face. The blows were so severe I thought I was going to die. One hard punch broke my nose. I was too shocked to scream for help. I had never been beaten so badly before. When I was young my mother used to pull my ears or cheeks when I was naughty and sometimes my parents would spank me on the bum. The only other time I got beaten was by my young brother, when he hit me in the stomach, or when my older siblings gave me a knock on the head, or mild slap across the face. But we were children. Now, it seemed, Daniel aimed to kill me and I didn't understand why. Perhaps I had said something that hurt him. In our argument, I told him that he was a useless drunk and I regretted having become involved with him. Harsh words.

No one could help me because our host was not too sure what was going on, although he heard sounds of scuffles in the room. When he tried to open the door, Daniel pushed the door back and locked it. He told him that we had had a small tiff and apologised for the disturbance. I was almost unconscious and desperate for help but couldn't talk or walk. I was bleeding severely from the nose. Daniel helped me to the bathroom and washed the blood from my face. He told me to go to bed and promised to take me to the doctor in the morning. I was in a lot of pain and eventually fell asleep.

When I woke up Daniel was gone. The whole place was quiet. I was weak, in pain and very swollen. Everyone had gone to church. I was confused. "How could Daniel do this to me? How could he go to church and carry on like everything was normal?" I wondered. But yes, that is what he wanted, to show his friend that everything was okay. He probably didn't realise how badly he had beaten me. I tried to cry but my eyes were too swollen, bruised and painful. I needed to see a doctor. I also couldn't understand how our lovely happy relationship suddenly turned so brutally sour. Years later when I opened up to my mother, she attributed Daniel's violence to witchcraft. I scoffed at her suggestion. I didn't believe in witchcraft at that stage. Years later, when strange things happened to me, I thought my mum's witchcraft suspicions could have been true.

I was not familiar with Cape Town and didn't know where to find a doctor. Besides, how was I to get there when I could barely walk? Blood started running down my legs. I had to act quickly. I called the emergency number. In no time, paramedics arrived. They said something might be wrong with the baby and they had to rush. The hospital was too far so they took me to a surgery nearby. I was immediately sedated to calm the pain.

I was woken up by my mobile phone ringing in my handbag. A nursing assistant walked into the room to check on me. She told me that the doctor would see me soon. The phone kept ringing so they advised me to turn it off. I was in no state to answer it. I needed to sleep, they said. There were eight missed calls from Daniel.

The doctor told me that I had lost the baby. I felt the bed on which I lay wobble. I was in a terrible state. I felt a sharp pain in my abdomen. My mind was on a roller coaster. What was I to do? I wanted my mother to comfort me; I wanted my friends, familiar faces; I tried to cry but was too weak. I wanted to get out of hospital and go home but the only home I had for now was the one I shared with the man who had done this to me. In fact, he was my only way out of Cape Town. I closed my eyes in the hope that this was just bad dream.

The doctor asked if I wanted him to phone anyone on my behalf. I refused. I was too ashamed to let anyone know about my situation. I thought they might laugh at me and spread rumours. I had been a victim of rumours before, so all I wanted was peace and quietness. I wanted to speak to my daughter but we'd sent her to a friend's place for the holiday and if I told her what had happened they'd find out about it. Besides, I didn't want her to know that I was hurting. Although I wanted Daniel to be punished for what he did to me, the thought of my family or friends seeing me all beaten up and helpless would have been embarrassing. Besides I still loved him and blamed myself for the beating I got from him.

But the doctor had to speak to someone about my condition because he needed to operate on me the following day to clean me up after I miscarried the baby. He needed a next-of-kin in case something went wrong. He asked me if he could phone Daniel. I wasn't sure. I was terrified of him. Surgery staff advised me to press charges against him for violent assault. They offered to phone the police to come to the clinic. The doctor even took photographs of my badly bruised body. One of my nasal bones was broken and I could not breathe properly. I got up to use the lavatory. I looked at myself in the mirror and was horrified at what I saw. I didn't recognise myself.

I couldn't stay at the clinic after the operation because I would have been charged for it. I didn't want to go back to where Daniel was. Surgery staff found a small bed and breakfast nearby where they took me. I was given medicine and told to get a lot of rest. When I woke up the following morning, I saw Daniel and his friend standing by my bedside. The sight of him disgusted me. I asked him to leave.

The next few days of my life were entirely in the hands of the man I despised so much for defacing me. As soon as I got better we flew back to Johannesburg. I felt trapped and stupid. I wanted to lay charges of assault against him. Daniel went on his knees and cried like a child as he begged for forgiveness. He promised never to lay a hand on me again. He said he loved me and didn't know why he hurt me so badly. I quickly forgave him.

The tension between me and Daniel's family continued. His brothers would insult me often. Daniel called them to order but they didn't stop. They just had to break us up. I spoke to my mother about my situation. I told her that I was fed up and wanted to end the engagement. She suggested it was too late because things had advanced and advised that I hang in there. I know she didn't really mean it. She loathed Daniel. She said he was not worthy of my hand in marriage. "Marriage is important my daughter. You don't want to be seen to be weak by walking out now. You'll please your enemies," she said. She assured me that things would get better after the wedding. I believed that my mother knew what she was talking about. After all, she had been married for more than thirty years, although she had walked out on my father.

But things didn't get better. One of Daniel's cousins wrote a letter to the entire family in Zambia urging them to unite against our marriage. They agreed to boycott the wedding and have nothing to do with him if he married me. Months before the wedding, I decided I had had enough. I would end the affair. My daughter and I moved out of Daniel's place. My friend offered us temporary accommodation. I packed my bags and left a note for him saying I was calling off the wedding. I wanted his family to be happy.

Later that evening Daniel drove to my friend's place. He picked me up so that we could discuss the matter at his house. When we got home, he locked the door and beat me up. There was no one at home to help me out. He whipped me with a belt, kicked me about, hit my head against the wall. He said that he was going to kill me because I was stupid. This time I was sure I was going to die. I passed out.

Daniel said he was sorry. He said that he had never beaten a woman before and he was not an abusive person. He put the blame on me. It was because I was stubborn and pompous that he beat me up. If I was humble like other women, he said, he'd never lay a finger on me. I believed him. I put the blame squarely on myself. He told me that I was a spoilt brat who thought too much of myself because I was famous. He said the reason his family didn't like me was because I was not good and humble like him. Again, I believed him. In fact I believed everything he said because I was

My International Career

I have had an illustrious and rewarding career with international media institutions and multilateral organisations. During my four year stint at the South African Broadcasting Corporation (SABC) in Johannesburg, I rose to the post of chief international correspondent. I traversed the world, mainly reporting on humanitarian and development issues, and civil wars and conflict in Africa. My passion for international affairs began at a very early age, from the time I represented all children in the Commonwealth, during the UN International Year of the Child in 1979. While at the SABC, I polished my skill in war reporting.

When I first requested to be assigned to cover the civil war in the Democratic Republic of Congo, then known as Zaire, my news editor and male colleagues scoffed. "You are a woman and won't survive that place. Besides you might break your nails carrying heavy equipment," they teased. I aimed to prove them wrong.

The Congolese conflict began in August 1998 and drew in nine African countries, as well as various rebel groups. The rumblings of war started as early as 1996, with the Rwandan government concerned about Hutu militia, Interehamwe, who had taken part in the genocide two years earlier and found themselves in refugee camps in the east of the then Zaire. Rwanda was concerned about Interehamwe regrouping and rearming. Kagame supported anti-Mobutu activities by the ethnic Congolese Tutsis called the Banyamulenge who had settled in the east of Zaire since the 1950s.

I went out into eastern Zaire in June 1998, the hotbed of the rebellion against President Mobutu Sese Seko. A few important rebel leaders had surfaced; Wamba dia Wamba, Zaid Ngoma and others. But prominent among them was Laurent Desire Kabila, leader of the strongest rebel group. My TV crew was looking for him for an interview. I had a way with information and news sources, which helped us track down Kabila at his hideout in Goma in north Kivu Province.

After waiting for nearly four hours to see him, we were led to his hideout. Kabila was a pleasant, plump gentleman, who welcomed me with a nice smile. His men had a tense air of security around them. I had to do a lot to assure him that I was merely a TV reporter wanting to hear his story and share it with the world. I also told him that I was Zambian. "Ah, I know

93

the country well. I once lived there. So you are my sister. Welcome." I had won him over!

We were only four minutes into our recording when his security men told me to stop. They had to get going. I was disappointed. There wasn't much substance in the interview. He'd begun by telling me about how bad things were in Zaire and how his government would improve life. "If only he had not wasted time by starting with all the silly comments about how he might consider taking you as a wife when he becomes president!" said my very irritated cameraman. I was just as annoyed. We couldn't do much. They had to leave. Later I was told by one of his men that the abrupt end to our interview was due to security reasons. They had to remain undetected in case of marauding pro-government fighters, but the truth is that Mobuto did not have a proper army which could have put up a fight against an organised group of militia. I felt bad about going back to Johannesburg with a half-baked story.

So I asked if my crew could be embedded with the rebel soldiers to wherever they were going. I was told that I was crazy. They were heading to Kisangani through the jungle and we could join them at our peril. They had already taken over the town of Kasega. We decided to tag along for a short distance. It would make good TV pictures. They agreed on condition that they confiscate our mobile phones and passports.

The rebels were also experts at propaganda. They seized every media opportunity. Allowing a TV crew to film them as they supposedly converged on the seat of government was to their gain. We followed behind in a four-wheel drive vehicle. Of course, they were not planning on getting there the conventional way. It was guerrilla warfare and various moves would be taken. But for the brief time we were with the rebels, we got the best recording any journalist could ever want.

Although Kabila's troops looked like a ragtag army, most of them young, in plain clothes and dressed in factory gumboots, they were well armed and well trained. And they didn't stick together. We followed one small group to which we were assigned.

They carried sophisticated war equipment; top of the range surface-to-air missiles, rocket launchers, Kalashnikovs, as well as satellite

94

communications and GPSs. I had to quickly acquaint myself with the type of weaponry to put my reporting into context. A simple rebel group in a remote part of the country should not have owned such equipment. There had to be a bigger force behind them - possibly the Rwandan and Ugandan regimes - as was alleged in other media and political circles.

The march from Kisangani was to be long and dangerous. Kabila's men had to remain undetected. After tracking them for about 200 kilometres in our four-by-four, we were told by one of their commanders to 'drop off'. "You have filmed enough now. Go back. You are disturbing us and we are now moving into dangerous territory." We didn't argue with them because we were struggling to keep up anyway.

There were also snakes, mosquitos and gorillas, and the prospect of being caught up in full-scale fighting was very strong. We had not planned this and had no back-up plan. During the filming, we would stay in the car and only get out to record when it was safe to do so. Much of the filming was shot through the windows of the vehicle. The rebels carried very few food supplies so when they got to a village they would attack, order young men to join the rebellion, and feed off the local villagers' chickens or goats. There was also a lot of killing and raping, although my TV crew did not actually witness this. But we later interviewed many rape victims.

War experts said that the rebellion by Kabila would not be too difficult until he approached Kinshasa. Mobutu had lost control of the east. He also did not have an army strong enough to repel the oncoming forces.

We got our phones and travel documents back, withdrew and drove hundreds of kilometres back to the town of Goma. It was approaching late evening and we had been warned about the dangers of the night in that region. We aimed to cross the border into Rwanda before it got dark. It was early evening when we got there. We spent the night in our rented vehicle which we handed back the following morning and flew to Entebbe, Uganda for our connecting flight back to South Africa. Despite not getting a good interview, we had a few nice visuals and a good story to tell.

Only a year earlier as a freelance reporter for M-Net's *Carte Blanche* programme, my TV crew and I had travelled the same route in search of Kabila and we were not able to interview him. This time around I did.

Less than a year after my meeting with Kabila and his Alliance of Democratic Forces for the Liberation of Congo-Zaire (ADFLC), I was back in his country. This time he had taken over power and had changed the country's name from Zaire, which it had been from 1971 to 1997, to the Democratic Republic of Congo. When Mobutu became president, he had replaced the name Congo with Zaire. The state's name derived from the Congo River, sometimes called *Zaire* by the Portuguese, adapted from the kiKongo word *nzere* or *nzadi* (river that swallows all rivers).

It was December 1998 and I was back in the DRC to report on yet another rebellion which had resulted in a civil war that pitched eight African countries plus other forces, for or against the government. Laurent Desire Kabila was facing an uprising from the east of the country, the same place where he had plotted his rebellion against Mobutu. Thousands of people had fled and were living as refugees in neighbouring countries. Thousands of others were killed. Kabila accused his former allies Rwanda and Uganda of supporting the rebellion so that they could plunder the mineral rich eastern part of the country. Ironically the two countries had helped him to power.

It was a dangerous time to be in Kinshasa. Victor, my cameraman and I suffered the consequences when a group of soldiers pounced on us while filming. On the day when Victor and I were arrested, we were caught secretly filming soldiers who were assaulting innocent civilians in the city centre. They brutally beat a man because he didn't stop when the presidential motorcade was passing. There were strict rules around that. Everybody had to park their vehicles to the side of the road, get out and stand still. Nobody could move, but some unsuspecting pedestrians who were approaching the main road from a dusty side walk were not aware that the presidential motorcade was driving by. Soldiers beat them severely soon after the president passed. Filming was forbidden during the war but I thought it was too good a visual to let go. Victor and I glanced at each other as if in agreement to tape the action. He slowly walked to his camera, pressed the record button and walked away from it so that they could not see that he was filming. A senior army officer known as *Le Commandant* spotted us and requested to view the tape that was in the camera recorder.

Victor quickly rewound it to the beginning where there were visuals of women at the market, children playing and an interview with the information minister. He hoped these would convince *Le Commandant* that we had not done anything wrong. But the soldier was patient. He watched the entire forty-two minutes of the tape recording through the camera lens until he saw visuals of his men whipping and kicking people. Victor and I were handcuffed and placed under arrest.

At first, we got bundled into an army truck with about a dozen soldiers. We were to be taken to the army headquarters to be charged. We begged to be driven there in our small hired vehicle which was chauffeured by a local Congolese national. We thought it safer and hoped that we could escape along the way and try to seek help from the Information Ministry, from where we had obtained permission to film. After loud arguments amongst the soldiers, *Le Commandant* allowed us to ride in our car but he and another soldier would come with us to ensure that we did not escape.

To our horror, we were not taken directly to the army barracks. Instead *Le Commandant* instructed the driver to take another route so that we could lose the truck full of soldiers which had been following us. We drove to an isolated place where army officers were drinking alcohol and dancing to loud music. It was only eleven o'clock in the morning but most of them were already drunk. The Congolese army was notorious for indiscipline. Victor and I were forced out of the car and ordered to buy beers for about ten soldiers who had joined us.

Le Commandant introduced me as his girlfriend. He also told his colleagues that my team was in very big trouble and it was entirely up to the soldiers to do what they wanted to us, but for the time being, I was his property. He spoke in the local dialect Lingala and sometimes branched into Swahili so I could pick up a few words. I was ordered to drink beer, at gunpoint. I looked at the bottle, it was a 1.5 litre *Primus*. I remember having tasted it about a year earlier in Kigali, after a few hard days of trying to track the then rebel leader, Kabila. But those were happier days than this one. I had no choice but to drink it, as the sweat-drenched soldier put his arms around me. In the meantime, the other soldiers robbed Victor, at gunpoint, of his wristwatch and gold chain. They also asked him for money. He quickly handed over a few hundred dollar notes, in the hope that this would set us free. It didn't. They wanted more money. We could not argue with them. They had guns, and had taken a lot of alcohol and smoked dagga or some other substance. We had to play along.

I had in my bag the bulk of the team's travel allowance and realised that the soldiers would take it all. I decided to hide some, just to enable us to get out of town when we got the chance. I asked to use the toilet. Inside the filthy lavatory, I quickly removed a few hundred dollars from my pouch and hid them in my bra. I thought of hiding some in my underwear, but it wasn't easy because I had jeans on. Before I could stash away all the money, *Le Commandant* kicked the rickety-rackety door open, angry that I was taking too long. He was drunk and had been smoking what Victor later told me was ganja or cannabis. He closed the door and tried to take off my clothes. I screamed, pushed him hard and ran out. Victor immediately realised what was going on. He ran towards me to help and begged for mercy. "Please don't do anything to her. Please we will give you anything. Take this camera instead. Don't hurt my friend." The drunken soldier was excited about the prospect of earning himself a fortune so he let me go. "Sit and buy *Pombe*," he ordered in very poor English. *Pombe* is the local name for alcohol. He was used to barking out orders. He was so drunk that he could barely stand still. He tried to carry the camera he had just been offered, but staggered with it. Victor willingly offered to help him; he had no intention of giving it up after all.

We went back to where the other soldiers were and continued buying alcohol for them. Victor kept the beers flowing until the little money in local currency he was left with ran out. I wondered whether we would get out of there alive. I wanted to cry but was too terrified.

Attempted sexual assaults on me were not a new thing - at school, at home by visiting male relatives and even at work. When I was younger I was afraid to report the attempts for fear of being reprimanded. Later, as I grew older and understood my rights, raising the alarm became much easier.

Victor and I repeatedly begged the soldiers to let us go or at least take us to the army barracks. We thought that way, we stood a better chance of safety or being set free. Two hours later, when the soldiers felt that they had had enough to drink, they drove us in our rented car to their headquarters.

We were locked in a tiny remand cell. There was dry urine and excrement on the floor. The stench was unbearable. We were ordered to remove our shoes and belts. I tore pages from my notebook and spread them on the floor of the cell so that we could step on them. It didn't help much. Victor handed me his socks. They didn't make much of a difference.

We stood in the tiny cell for almost an hour. We were tired and dehydrated from all the beers we had been forced to drink. Our bottled water ran out and we dared not risk drinking the local tap water. I was tired. I wanted to sit down but couldn't. But the smell and filth of our cell faded out of our minds. We realised this might be our home for a while to come. We had to get used to it.

The cell was in an isolated building and Victor kept saying that he was sure the soldiers would kill him and do something bad to me. I was more hopeful and suggested we pray. Then we heard voices and footsteps. Some men were approaching. We didn't know whether to be happy or afraid. Unruly soldiers in a state of war are unpredictable.

A superior-looking soldier with two others accompanied by *Le Commandant* approached the tiny cell. He gave an order in French. It was the first time I heard any of the soldiers speak French, the country's official language. The two saluted and opened the cell door. He beckoned to Victor and me to come out and follow him to his office. He did not speak much. He had a big scar on his face and looked very tough. There appeared to be more order to him though. This was the first sign of hope for us.

Le Commandant who appeared to have sobered up a bit handed over our case to other army officers. Our prayer was that he would not take the camera. He didn't. He gave in the equipment and the video tape as well. We were relieved. Perhaps he realised that a professional TV 'digicam' would not be of much use to him or anyone else. Our driver in the meantime was in his vehicle outside the barracks. He was told not to say a word about the day's incident or he and his family would be killed. They had his home address and driving license.

The senior army man wrote down our details. He asked us our names, where we were born, the names of our parents, our grandparents and where they were born. The ink in his pen ran out. I quickly took one out from my pouch and offered it to him. He looked up and smiled at me. I smiled back. Then he read out the charges in French. He said we were being charged for spying for a foreign power. He did not state which power though. Kabila had accused the South African government of supporting the rebellion against him, charges which were never proven. So a South African TV crew in Kinshasa was obviously treated with suspicion. The army officer said we had committed a very serious offence for which we would be jailed for a long time, or even executed if the court found us guilty.

My mind began to race. I thought about my children and my life back home in Johannesburg. Was this it? Is this how my adventurous and happy life would end? "No!" I said loudly and began to explain myself in basic French. "We are not spies. We are journalists. See this letter from your information minister? He knows us. We were with him yesterday. Please phone him." I said a lot of things. I had to save my life and that of Victor, who turned to the soldier and said, "Look at me, I am Mandela's brother. If you kill me, you will hurt Mandela." I thought it was a stupid thing to say, but at that stage, anything to save our lives counted. I also realised at that moment that indeed Victor did resemble Mandela. But that didn't matter now. We had to stay alive. I took out my Zambian passport and showed it to the soldier. He was stony-faced.

My colleague and I offered to plead guilty to filming without permission and pay a fine. "How much do you have?" asked the soldier calmly. I told him that I had a bit of money. He said he would take it quickly before the others came in and let us go, but we were not to say word to anyone about the payment.

I remembered that the money was still stashed in my bra. I couldn't take it out in the army office, so just as I did when I figured to hide the money, I requested to use the toilet urgently. It was a daring request for the army barracks' toilets were not fit for human use. Instead of going into the smelly pit latrine which was shielded by metal roofing sheets on all sides, I went behind one of the buildings, quickly took the money from my bra and ran back in the officer's room. I gave him US$200. His face lit up.

That was probably equivalent to his monthly salary.

He set Victor and me free and ordered us to leave immediately. He confiscated our video tape but gave us back the camera. *Le Commandant* had left by now and we were delighted. We had never moved faster in our lives. We ran out of the main gate, got into the waiting vehicle and rushed from the scene, lest *Le Commandant* and others show up and try to extort money from us, or worse. It was going on towards late afternoon. Kinshasa was a dangerous place at night and the driver told us that our hotel was about an hour's drive. We did not say a word to each other on the way. As soon as we got there, Victor mounted the satellite link on the roof of the hotel, I called the SABC newsroom in Johannesburg to quickly narrate what had happened and we were lined up for a recorded interview to lead the evening news at 7 p.m.

Ours was a breaking news story, for earlier in the day, the broadcast station had reported us missing because they had lost touch with us the whole day. It was standard practice to maintain communication with the newsroom when we were out on a dangerous mission. We had not been able to. *Le Commandant* confiscated our phones when we were arrested. I spent the next thirty minutes doing various radio and TV interviews about what had happened during the day.

That night my then-husband phoned and ordered me to return home as soon as possible. He was very angry and worried. I ignored him. I had unfinished business in the DRC and only then would I go back home. As I lay in bed that night, I realised just how much I loved my job. One thing bothered me though. During breakfast the following morning, I said to Victor, "Shouldn't taking a hot shower have been the first thing we did when we got back to the hotel yesterday?" Victor gave me a rather puzzled look. The fact is, we didn't do that. Instead, we phoned headquarters to tell our story first, then we cleaned ourselves up!

Following our incident, we noticed armed security outside our hotel rooms. We were not sure if they were there to protect us or to watch us. There was an official complaint from the South African Foreign Ministry about what had happened to us, so the Congolese government ensured

101

that a police officer would accompany us for the duration of our stay. But despite this, there were several attempts to arrest us everywhere we went.

Two days later, my request for an exclusive interview with President Kabila was granted. We had to be at the presidential palace by 8 a.m. for a press conference, after which I'd do the interview. It was another tedious experience. Security was extremely tight. Vehicles were not allowed in the president's compound. We parked our cars kilometres away and had to walk the distance to the state house.

There were about three layers of security checks. We were body searched. We could not take in anything, except our notebooks and pens. Our equipment was scrutinized. Items such as lipstick, perfume or other make-up could not go in, lest they contained poison. It took more than an hour to search all of us. We waited another two hours before the president appeared to address us. While we were waiting for him, I spotted *Le Commandant*, the drunken soldier who had arrested Victor and me. I gave him a stern look and wagged my finger at him, to indicate that I was going to report him. He smiled and gave me a friendly wave. I told Victor that I was going to point him out to the president as the man who had harassed us, stolen our money and even tried to rape me. My blood was boiling. My colleague didn't think it a good idea. As if he sensed my intentions, *Le Commandant* quickly made his way to where Victor and I were, and beckoned us to follow him outside. The look on his face changed when we got outside and in a low slow tone of voice he said to me, "One word and we kill driver and all family. I kill ehh!" That was it. I reluctantly kept my mouth shut.

During the press conference and later that afternoon when I interviewed President Kabila, he appeared tired and dejected. He wasn't the same vibrant rebel leader whom I had met months earlier in Goma. He gave a wide-ranging interview in which he complained about external interference in his government. He denied allegations that his soldiers were killing the Banyamulenge as reprisals for what he alleged were attempts to unseat him by President Kagame and Museveni. Mr Kabila also complained about what he termed the South African government's turnaround support for his administration.

The country had not had multiparty elections since the 1960s when Patrice Lumumba was elected prime minister, though later shot by firing squad in January 1961, following an army mutiny and subsequent secessionist activities of the Katanga rebels in the south of the country. Belgium, the United Kingdom, and the United States were accused of involvement in Lumumba's death. Kabila referred to himself as 'Lumumbist', committed to holding democratic elections as soon as the peace came into force. "But," he said to me, "I am not sure if I'll be here for long." I asked him what he meant. "They might want to kill me," he said. He had an air of resignation about him. That was in December 1998. On 16th January 2001, Laurent Kabila Desire was assassinated. I had left the SABC by then and was getting ready for my next post at the BBC. I would have liked to go back to Kinshasa to cover the story, although it was an extremely dangerous phase.

There were various versions of his assassination, including one that he was killed by one of his bodyguards. Rashidi was alleged to be part of an elaborate international conspiracy again by Belgium, the US, Britain, Rwanda and Uganda to kill Kabila. But according to an article by Stuart Jeffries of the UK Guardian, published on 11 February 2001, Kabila's *kadogos* (Swahili for 'child soldiers') committed patricide against a man they believed to have betrayed them. Kabila's young killer entered the president's office at the Marble Palace in Kinshasa on 16 January, as Kabila was discussing with an economic adviser a pending summit with France, which he hoped would be his political salvation. The assassin bent over Kabila, and the president, assuming the teenager wanted to talk to him, leaned towards him. The *kadogo* produced a revolver and shot the president four times, then escaped with other conspirators while the palace resounded with gunfire.

Official reports were that Kabila was rushed to Zimbabwe with the hope of saving his life. Mugabe was a strong ally of the DRC and they didn't trust anyone in Kinshasa at the time of the shooting. But he is said to have succumbed to his gunshot wounds on board the plane.

My love affair with Kinshasa did not end there. I went back in 2004, when I took a sabbatical from the BBC, to work for the UN Peace Keeping

Mission known as MONUC, from September to December 2004. The vibrant city had changed since the last time I was there in 1998. The war had ended and there were reconstruction and peace building efforts by various national and international groups.

My role as public information officer was to disseminate information on what the UN peacekeeping mission was doing and to inform the local population about the mission as well as post conflict development efforts.

A few weeks after I got to Kinshasa, civil servants rioted and there were attacks on UN vehicles and staff houses. They had been misinformed that the UN was the cause of their not being paid their salaries. One of our vehicles was torched and we spent two nights in our offices at the secure UN compound in Gombe. We were prepared for the occasion. Part of our security briefing when we arrived in the DRC was to have a 'to-go bag' ready. This small bag, weighing no more than five kilograms, consisted of a wrapper or cloth to sleep on or cover ourselves, biscuits, torch, spare phone or battery and water, in case war broke out and we had to escape to a place without basic amenities. It was a survival kit. I've always kept one ready ever since.

"Shooting" the War in Sierra Leone

It was a tense and exciting morning for my family in August 1999. In the last three years, I had travelled to a number of African countries to report on elections, social and humanitarian issues, politics and conflict. My children were too young to fully comprehend what my TV news reports were about but they were happy and proud to see their mother on television.

I had always wanted to report on conflict from the time when my father, also a journalist, told me stories about his adventurous reporting in war zones such as Zaire, Algeria, Vietnam, Gibraltar, Lebanon and Nigeria. He also spoke fondly about his days as a freedom fighter in Zambia and how he and others fearlessly fought the racist and brutal British colonial system. I was proud of him and wanted to follow in his footsteps.

I was tense on this particular day because I was scheduled to leave for Freetown in Sierra Leone to report on the protracted and dangerous civil war. I had heard terrifying things about what was happening in the fighting, which pitted the rebel Revolutionary United Front (RUF) of Foday Sankoh, a former army corporal against the government of President Ahmed Tidjan Kabbah. The civil war began in 1991 with Sankoh's campaign against previous President Joseph Momoh, capturing towns on the border with Liberia. His RUF forces became notorious for brutal practices such as mass rapes, amputations and murder.

There had also been a series of military coups, about four within a space of three years. The Economic Community of West African States Monitoring Group (ECOMOG) was a multilateral armed force established by West African States. They were credited with playing a big part in ending the fighting in Sierra Leone. Other players were the UN and British troops. A ceasefire was agreed in 1999, and some rebels from the RUF were given government posts. Child soldiers were heavily recruited in the war; a total of 11,000 are thought to have participated in the conflict. Most were used for attacks on villages and on guard duty at diamond fields, as well as guarding weapons stockpiles. Security experts said that the RUF was armed and supported by former Liberian President Charles Taylor to cause social and political upheaval to enable the plunder of the valuable diamonds in Sierra Leone. Years later, this was argued conclusively at the International Criminal Court at The Hague, which found Taylor guilty in

April 2012, on eleven counts of crimes against humanity including murder, enslavement, rape, and the recruitment of child soldiers. The following month he was sentenced to fifty years in prison. He is serving his sentence in a British jail.

The story of the conflict in 1999 was a big one, often told from the perspective of western media. In a way, I was proud of the important task entrusted to me.

The flight to Abidjan was at midday. It was a full flight because South African Airways was one of the few airlines flying to Ivory Coast and the West African region. Others had to fly as far as Frankfurt, Amsterdam or Paris to connect to a city in West Africa.

My cameraman, Pat and I had a lot of equipment to carry so we checked in early. Then a big row broke out between us over the 'gear', a TV term for filming equipment. We couldn't agree on how best to handle it.

I phoned my assignment editor to ask that he speak to Pat before we left, to ensure that he understood that I was the boss. The producer is always in charge, but it seemed Pat had a problem with that. In no time, the editor was on the phone with my colleague. As soon as he hung up Pat walked up to me to apologise. I was still sulking. I hated being undermined and ensured that we were not seated together on the flight.

The six-and-a half hour journey was smooth and comfortable. When we got to Abidjan, Pat apologised again. He said that we would be spending a week or more together on a very dangerous assignment and the least we could do was get along. I agreed with him and we hugged, as a sign of a truce. It turned out later that we had argued because we were both very nervous about the upcoming mission.

We got to Abidjan late in the evening. We were to connect to Freetown the following morning on Ghana Airways via Accra. We checked into a hotel and had a good meal. Pat advised me to enjoy the last moments of comfort and good food before we set off to the war zone.

In Accra our connecting flight was delayed for more than three hours. "It is typical of Ghana Airways to be late," said one irate passenger. He worked for the United Nations in Freetown. Pat and I were concerned that if we got to our destination very late, we would miss the helicopter ride to the mainland. The UN and a few private helicopters were the only means of transport from the small island airport at Lungi to Freetown, but did not fly after 6 p.m. for security reasons. We had to stick to the plan. Our main contact in Freetown was a Mr Kwame at the UN and we needed to catch him before he knocked off. We had a few other contacts such as journalists, but we thought the UN would be more reliable.

We were in luck. We landed at Lungi airport about twenty minutes before the next helicopter was due to leave. We had to be very quick. The TV gear was heavy but with the help of young men loitering about, we managed to get it on board. The thirty minute flight to Freetown was US$100 per person. The sky was clear, but I was nervous, especially when we flew over the Atlantic Ocean to get to the other side.

I prayed all the way until we landed. Then we hired a local driver, Mohammed to take us to our hotel. We didn't have a reservation and were horrified to learn that there were no functional hotels at all in Freetown. They had all been destroyed in the fighting. *Mamiyoko*, which was once a prestigious five-star hotel, was now a bombed-out shell in which RUF rebels sometimes hid or lodged with their wives and children, girlfriends or prostitutes.

The only decent place available, recommended by the UN, was the Cape Sierra. Under the circumstances, it was not too bad. We were tired and needed to get some rest before our task ahead.

The following day, we had fruit juice and some biscuits which we had carried from Johannesburg. We'd not risk eating food whose hygiene standards we were not sure of. There were water-borne diseases such as cholera. I had also heard allegations that some places sold dog meat due to food shortages. There were a lot of stray dogs in Freetown so catching one for a meal, if it was true that they served as food, would not have been a big mission. The rebels were reported to have eaten human flesh, a ritual meant to make them fiercer. There were also rumours that some of this flesh found itself in meat stews to compensate for the shortage of meat products. All this might have been propaganda, but I wouldn't take the risk.

Mr Kwame at the UN office was not very helpful. He was cranky and irritable. When I had spoken to him before we got to Freetown he'd offered to link us up with important news sources. But now he said he was too busy to assist. There was a lot going on in the country. Interviewing the main rebel leader, Foday Sankoh or any of the other militia leaders was an important part of our story. I was known for the big scoops, but this one was different. A lot of people were baying for Sankoh's blood and it was impossible to find him.

We interviewed UN officials, commanders of the British troops and ECOMOG, as well as some government representatives. But the real story was on the ground among the people, life in the city and how the locals were getting on after months of clashes.

Sierra Leone was ranked the world's poorest country by the World Bank. Most parts of the capital city were rusty, dilapidated and unflattering. Hospitals could not cope with the rate of daily casualties and those suffering the consequences of the war such as malnutrition and disease. The country also had the highest number of mentally ill people in the world. It is estimated that 715,000 people suffered from civil war-related mental illness.

Mohammed, the hired driver, took us to a centre for victims of the war. There were people with chopped limbs, severed lips and noses, and no ears. Rebel soldiers did this to them. "They said that if they chopped off our hands, we would not be able to vote for President Kabbah," said Moktar, the spokesperson for the war victims.

Even babies were not spared. These were sad but 'good' images for TV. Victims spoke of their horror and suffering. "Each time I go to the toilet, my wife has to help me clean myself up. I am worse than an animal," said a man who had lost both arms. Many girls and young women were abducted and taken as wives or sex slaves. The camp was littered with children, born of raped women. Some spoke of how they were forced to chop off the arms or fingers of their own children or parents. Women spoke of watching their husbands killed while men told shocking stories of how they were forced to watch their wives, mothers or sisters being sexually violated. There was a deep sense of helplessness. Pat and I captured it all on tape.

But the situation was too much for Pat. He couldn't bear it. He put his camera down and burst into tears. He was inconsolable. I was angry and embarrassed. I didn't expect a grown man to cry in front of his subjects. Pat had covered dangerous and difficult stories, but it seems this one overwhelmed him. I instructed him to get up, gave him a bottle of water and asked him to continue shooting. My frequent reporting of these issues had desensitized me to pain and suffering. It was as if my feelings had been eternally numbed. I never cried, although I was to be haunted years later by the horrors I had seen in my war reporting.

We were also taken to a rebel hideout where the fighters gave their own version of the conflict. They demanded jobs and money as well as inclusion in the government, as a condition to lay down arms. "Pipo na propaganda na dey talk. We won mone. If they don give mone, we go inside bush and we dey come kill," said one of their leaders in the local Creole dialect.

Four days into our Sierra Leone mission, I heard someone call my name. Surprised, I turned to see two men in UN uniforms bearing small Zambian flags on the pocket and shoulder. They said they recognised me from TV back home. I was very happy and immediately engaged them in an off-record conversation about life in Freetown. They were not authorised to speak on record but they gave us an informed perspective of the political situation and the war in general and linked Pat and me to vital news makers.

In the evening we joined the Zambian soldiers for dinner at a restaurant said to be the best in town. It did not offer much, but most foreigners dined there. They said the food was fresher and clean. That was the first proper meal my cameraman and I had in four days. We had survived on biscuits, fruit juices, potato crisps and chocolates. We now felt secure among my country's troops. But we were warned that if serious fighting broke out, our safety would not be guaranteed. We'd be on our own.

We restricted our reporting to Freetown for security reasons. A few days after our arrival, we went into the infamous 'seven day rainfall' period, an annual feature in August, when the rain falls for seven days straight, without interruption.

One morning, word went around that the shaky peace deal had ended and fighting had broken out. There were also rumours of rebel forces approaching the outskirts of Freetown. At first, Pat and I paid little attention to the story, but word got stronger by midday. None of our news sources could tell us exactly what was going on. I got the impression that I was beginning to irritate the British troops' spokesperson and the others that I contacted all the time for first-hand information. But that was my job, to get the information, even if I irritated them.

By now it was pouring heavily and we were not able to film properly. We couldn't file stories home either because of the poor satellite signal. With the security situation uncertain and no guarantee of our safety if attacks happened, Pat and I decided to get out.

We had to find our way to the airport to catch a helicopter to Lungi, then wait for a connecting flight to Accra. Ghana Airways was the only airline flying to and from Sierra Leone, albeit once a week on Thursdays. This was Tuesday and we needed to get out. The UN informed me that none of their helicopters were flying for fear of being shot at by RPGs (rocket propelled grenades) or surface-to-air missiles. Using our satellite phone, I called the SABC in Johannesburg for advice. We couldn't communicate. Luckily one of the Zambian troopers lent me his phone. The editor told us to get out in whatever way we could. But with no flight leaving, it seemed we were trapped. Our only hope was to seek protection from the UN for the next two days until we were able to catch the next flight. UN soldiers and other peace keepers had been attacked and kidnapped before, so the troops from Zambia warned us that if the UN was hit, we too would be in the firing line.

Then word came in that a Russian private plane was leaving from a small airstrip in Freetown for Conakry in Guinea. Those who wanted to flee had to be at the airport quickly, because it was leaving in less than an hour. I did not blink. We loaded our gear into Mohammed's Peugeot 404 and rushed to the airstrip. When I saw the plane, I was not sure whether to board the aircraft or turn back and face the onslaught of the approaching rebels, if at all they were coming to town.

It was a 1970s Tupolov with propellers. Pat suggested we get on. The ride to Conakry was US$30. The seats which looked like benches were made of wood. Windows were covered by dirty and dusty faded curtains hung across with a wire. They stank so much that I had to cover my nose for the entire thirty minute flight.

The plane's engine could only start after being wound by a Russian engineer outside on the nose of the aircraft, by something that looked like a

110

spanner. Soon we were on our way. A very tall Russian cabin attendant, the only one on board the 26-seater, went around collecting money for the fare. She was so tall that she crouched forward as she walked down the aisle. Pat and I could not stop sniggering. We had to. It calmed our nerves and helped us cope with the fright of being on a very old, scary airplane.

When we landed in Conakry, everyone on board clapped and cheered. We were happy to be out of danger. But Conakry airport posed another challenge. People, mostly women, walked up to the tarmac to help disembarking passengers with their luggage. The airport was crowded and rowdy. The locals were imposing and ill-mannered, grabbing women's handbags without their permission.

"They don't have a proper luggage handling system here so groups of people walk to the aircraft as soon as the door opens to carry bags to the airport terminal for a fee. A lot of bags go missing so be careful," cautioned a man on the flight. But Pat and I had no choice. We had heavy equipment and needed someone to help us carry it to a taxi.

My basic knowledge of French was very useful. The taxi driver took us to a good hotel. We had not taken a proper bath in days. Hot water in Freetown was rare and some days there was no water at all. I met with Pat in the restaurant after spending nearly twenty minutes in the shower. We treated ourselves to a sumptuous Senegalese fish meal.

The next day, we got a flight to Abidjan then connected to Johannesburg in the afternoon. Two days after we landed back home, Sierra Leone made the global news headlines: rebel forces had marched onto towns on the outskirts of the capital and attacked a number of UN troops. A UN contingent of peacekeepers from Zambia was caught off guard, hit like sitting ducks. Twenty three of the troops were killed, including the two men whom Pat and I met in the streets and who had taken us to a decent restaurant and assisted us with contacts.

I knelt, prayed and cried. I was nominated for the coverage in journalism award by the International Women Media Fund, as well as for a CNN Award. But I didn't win. It didn't matter. The experience was worth it. And it certainly wasn't the last time I reported on conflict.

My BBC Career

I thought I was dreaming when I got a call from the respected Robin White of Focus on Africa to invite me for a phone interview and audition for a job on the BBC World Service.

My first assignment in February 2001, while waiting to get my UK work permit, was to interview former President Chiluba on whether he was planning to circumvent the constitution so that he could run for a third term. The nation wanted to hear from him. There'd been speculation for months that he would run. His second five-year term was coming to an end. He was silent on the matter and the public wanted to know. "What better place for them to hear it than the BBC," I thought.

Through my networks, I secured the interview with the president and flew to Lusaka. It was a pleasure to be back at State House, the place where I got my first crash course in reporting from President Kaunda, fifteen years earlier. It is also the place where I did my last assignment before I finally left Zambia. I attended President Chiluba's cabinet reshuffle press conference in 1992. I asked him a question about the Zambian Government's relations with the Africa National Congress of South Africa. He was a bit rattled by the question but answered it candidly. "Well, the ANC gave strong support to UNIP and Dr Kenneth Kaunda ...." he rambled on. I had heard from my sources that the ANC was not too pleased with Mr Chiluba and the MMD because their election campaign in 1991 was allegedly bankrolled by the apartheid government. "The logic of it", said my ANC source, "was that KK was a thorn in the flesh of the de Klerk administration and that of his predecessor P.W. Botha as well as others before."

Dr Kaunda was leader of the frontline states. Zambia hosted refugees and political exiles from liberation movements including SWAPO of Namibia, Frelimo of Mozambique, ZAPU from Zimbabwe and South Africa's ANC. The former Zambian leader also worked tirelessly through international efforts and other clandestine methods to bring about the independence of these countries. It would have made sense for the racist regime to support any opposition movement against Kaunda.

I felt welcome at State House and I was offered tea with fritters, President Chiluba's favourite tea accompaniment. We had a wide-ranging interview in which he disclosed that he had at no time stated that he'd run for a third term. He didn't put it any other way and for me that was a big story. The BBC ran it as headline news and the agitation and manoeuvring in the MMD over succession began to unravel. That was yet another big scoop and a great entry point into the BBC!

I must say that even if I had been to London on brief visits before, living there was a cultural shock. I rented a friend's council flat in the south of London. The place was awash with immigrants many from West Africa and the West Indies. On the morning when I arrived in London, I took a shower then slept. I woke up in the afternoon in total shock, when I peeped through the window. My flat was above East Street, which was a market street. Every Tuesday, vendors would sell their merchandise ranging from fruits and vegetables to clothes, shoes, meat and other goods, on the street, and very cheaply. I saw more black faces than white ones. Having lived in South Africa, I had become more colour conscious. The streets were filthy and the walls were covered in graffiti. The place looked drab. For a moment, I thought I was lost. Could this be London or had I got onto the wrong plane? I moved out of the area after six months.

I enjoyed working for the BBC. It was intense, hard work involving long tedious shifts. I started with Network Africa, a popular breakfast news and current affairs show. It was hard. The shift would start at 10 p.m. and end at 9 a.m. the following day, with five intense thirty minutes' shows starting at 03.30 GMT. That's the time I was used to going to bed. I struggled and the show suffered. I was low key, boring and tired and my editors were not impressed. They also wanted me to change my formal newsy way of presenting to the slightly laid-back, magazine breakfast format that Network Africa was. I couldn't do it. I was a hard news journalist. I remember my father telling me after one of my programmes that my show was 'OK'. This was a polite way of him saying my performance was mediocre.

Adjusting to my new life was also difficult. I had to jump on the bus or 'tube' (underground train) to go to work and everywhere else I went. Back home I had a car. In London, I lived in a small flat with no garden. In Johannesburg I had a beautiful big house, a pool, with an English country garden. In London, I also had a lot of personal problems relating to my marriage which made it hard for me to focus on my new job.

Later, I was moved to *Focus on Africa*, a programme which suited my presentation style and sleeping pattern. My work started improving and I began to enjoy what I was doing. The experience I gained at the BBC was immeasurable. I was trained in all aspects of broadcasting. I was privileged to work with world class journalists from whom I learned a lot. Again, I travelled and reported from other countries, although my main mandate was to produce and present Focus on Africa from London. I can proudly say that I grew the audiences from Southern Africa, with hundreds of thousands of my local fans tuning in to the BBC. I also played a significant role in churning out editorial content and delivery of news and current affairs on the World Service. It brought pride and honour to my family and to me. One of my biggest achievements at the BBC was my part in negotiating with the Zambian government to transmit our programmes on FM in 2002. Before then, the BBC could only be heard on a crackly shortwave band which was not always clear.

My Passion for Conflict Reporting

In 2007, after I left the BBC, I was asked by my former employers the SABC to cover the contentious Kenyan general elections. I didn't blink! It was as though being in the midst of fire was addictive. People questioned how my seemingly soft and calm persona survived in the heat of bombs, tear gas and all sorts of violence, as the Kenyan elections proved to be. Perhaps it is just that; my calm and deceivingly soft persona gets me through difficult situations. In truth, I am very brave and have exceptional will power. They also asked me why I covered hard stories. My response: the truth had to be told, from an African perspective.

My story for the day took me to the thick of conflict in the Kibera slum of Nairobi the biggest slum in Africa, where I'd gone to report on the electoral process. It was one of the areas affected by the violence following disputed elections in 2007 in which President Mwai Kibaki, a Kikuyu, was re-elected.

Our news crew was accosted by local dwellers who wanted me out of the place because they said I was a Kikuyu. The population of Kibera is predominantly Luo or Luhya and they supported the main opposition leader Raila Odinga. The irate residents of Kibera insisted that I was Kikuyu and I was ordered to leave. I was almost beaten up. In my effort to prove that I wasn't Kenyan, I took out my Zambian passport to show them and opened the first page. Big mistake. My middle name is Mumbi, which means creator or mother of the tribe in my language and in Kikuyu.

I hastily left Kibera under police escort.

Then there was a news media blackout when election results were due. This incensed part of the population which suspected vote rigging. I recall spending Christmas in my hotel room because it was too dangerous to venture out. All shops and restaurants were closed. There was not much food at the hotel either because there were no deliveries of fresh supplies for fear of attacks. I sat in my room for two days watching foreign news reports on the elections and snacking on dried fruits, crisps and biscuits which I'd carried from Johannesburg. It was always a rule among SABC journalists to carry non-perishable food from home because we were not too sure what we'd find where we were going. Often this helped.

I evolved into a tough, hard-nosed Africa specialist. I interviewed presidents, including Zambia's former leaders Kaunda, Chiluba, and

Mwanawasa, as well other world leaders and politicians. But I also spoke to anyone who had a story to tell.

Among the fascinating interviews I conducted was one with the President of Somaliland who walked out of the SABC studio because he didn't like my line of questioning; or when the camera light blew up and nearly fell on former President Kaunda during an interview in Cape Town. Then there was *Mama 50 Naira* who owned a food store on the streets of Lagos. She sold delicious food, at fifty Naira a plate. But she had a lot more to offer than a good dish. She was an excellent source of news. I don't know where she got her information from but she knew what was happening, who was involved and why. She even had phone numbers of politicians and businessmen. I often paid more than just 50 Naira for the plate of food. I also paid for the juicy bits, most of which were off the record.

Upmost on my mind was my news coverage of former South African President Nelson Mandela, or Tata Madiba as he was affectionately known. Our SABC TV crew flew to Abuja in 1999 for the inauguration of former Nigerian President Olusegun Obasanjo. My cameraman and I door-stepped (unplanned interview) President Obasanjo when he escorted Madiba to the airport soon after the swearing in ceremony. Although Mr Obasanjo was not too keen on giving the interview, President Mandela calmly and kindly asked him to grant us a few words. SABC was the only TV crew that got a sound bite directly from the newly-sworn in Nigerian leader, thanks to Madiba's intervention. We had to pipe the story to Johannesburg right away. We had a big scoop. To my disgust, my cameraman struggled with the *Tokobox*, a digital satellite transmission system and sadly we missed out of filing first class sound bites and pictures. If it had been up to me I would have fired him there and then.

What was also interesting about the Abuja assignment was that it was a significant occasion marking a new political process in Nigeria. Global leaders were flying to Abuja for the swearing-in ceremony. Air traffic was a nightmare. Our TV crew was in a commercial aircraft carrying some of Madiba's personal security. He was on a flight a few minutes ahead of ours with only two of his physical security and some of his assistants. The directive from airport control in Abuja was that no plane was to land

118

until Madiba's plane had landed. His security team on our flight said that was not going to happen because they had to be on the ground before Mandela's plane touched down. There was an argument between ground control and the team on board while our plane circled around. Twice we were forced to land and take off from Kano, then Kaduna airport, before finally landing, two-and-a-half hours later. Only after his security team had taken position did Madiba's plane touch down. That's how great that man was! A few years later, while covering the South African elections for the BBC in 2006, I again met Madiba at the FNB football stadium during the final ANC election rally. He was driven in a golf cart around the stadium to ballistic applause from the packed audience. Former president Thabo Mbeki was with him and the world's press ran beside and after the golf cart like hungry hyenas, to try and get a photo or sound bite from Madiba. I was very close to him and about to stick my microphone at him with a question when his security pushed me off. The pleasures of journalism!

Prior to President Obasanjo taking the oath of office, I'd gone to Lagos to cover the elections, which Obasanjo won with 62.78% of the vote. This was the first democratic poll in sixteen years so it was a big story. I wanted an interview with the president-elect as did all other journalists.

A reliable source tipped me on the day the results were announced that Mr Obasanjo would be in his home town of Abeokuta in the south of the country. The source also confirmed the interview. My team and I quietly sneaked out of Lagos for Abeokuta. And we were in luck, Mr Obasanjo was there. We were told to wait, and we did.

Unfortunately, word got around that the president-elect was in Abeokuta. Soon, a trail of cars rode up the dust road to the newly elected leader's farm. They were mostly international journalists from Reuters, CNN, BBC and others. I didn't want competition and I didn't want to share the interview either. I want exclusivity.

After an hour of waiting his staff announced that Obasanjo would give an exclusive interview to SABC. We followed him to the room where Mr Obasanjo was waiting. Other journalists would not have it. They blocked the entrance to the room. "You cannot give SABC this big interview," said one former Reuters and later CNN correspondent. He complained that there were bigger news networks that deserved the interview. I was livid.

I tried to push my way through rival journalists. We shoved, pushed and scuffled as Nigeria's newly elected president watched, in total horror. His security stepped in quickly to stop the madness. President Obasanjo got up, and angrily told us to go away. He said we were disrespectful and badly behaved and he'd not give any of us the interview. I refused to leave. After waiting for about twenty minutes the other journalists left. I stayed put. I was not going anywhere until I'd done the interview. After the lot had left, Mr Obasanjo stepped out of his house to get into the car. He was now going to Abuja. I ran towards him with my crew. The camera and recorder were switched on, I pointed the microphone towards him and began asking him questions. He had no choice but to respond. The interview was short and rushed, but I got the main elements.

In addition to President Obasanjo, I interviewed many presidents, world and business leaders. I remember an embarrassing moment at the UN General Assembly in 1999. The conflict in Sierra Leone was on the agenda of the Security Council. My big news target was Sir Jeremy Greenstock, the Permanent Representative of the United Kingdom to the UN. Britain had troops in Sierra Leone. They played a significant role in peace-keeping efforts. I secured the interview with him and was well prepared. I knew the subject well so I didn't write down the questions or talking points. The room was packed with senior UN and British diplomats, security staff and journalists. I was at the centre of it all. Five minutes into the interview my mind went blank. I couldn't remember what to ask next, or what he had just said. I stammered and stuttered for a minute, mumbled a few senseless words, then was forced to apologise for the loss in my train of thought. He was kind enough to agree to start the interview over again. I was extremely embarrassed.

Perhaps the most memorable highlight of my journalism career was in July 1998, when I reported on the bombing of the US Embassies in Dar-es-Salaam and Nairobi, by Al-Qaida. I was off duty when the two embassies were attacked. My editor at the SABC phoned to ask if I could go. CNN was chartering a cargo plane to Dar-es-Salam, and I could ride along that afternoon. The adrenaline kicked in. Within an hour, I had packed and was headed for the airport.

The cargo flight to Dar was long and uncomfortable. As soon as we landed, we rushed to the hotel to drop off our luggage and in no time we were filming at the site of the bombing, doing interviews and attending briefings by the Tanzanian and US governments' spokespersons. The second day my editor wanted me to appear on camera - to do what we call in TV a 'piece to camera' or link. I couldn't. My breasts were full of milk. They hurt and the milk was oozing. I was in pain, irritable and restless. I had pumped several bottles of milk for my baby son before I left but the milk in me kept flowing. I was confused. I wanted to do the big story but felt the need to go back home. On the fourth day of my assignment, a replacement from Johannesburg took over the reporting and I flew back home.

I also travelled a lot to Zambia to report on alleged UNITA activities in north western Zambia. There were allegations that senior officials in the defence ministry were providing military and logistical support in the form of a launch base, to UNITA leader Jonas Savimbi and his troops. It was a difficult story to prove but I was determined to find out. It was important to know whether this support was personal, or came as government backing. Angola's former ambassador to Zambia cautioned the Zambian government about this. "Zambian territory is being used to supply arms to UNITA, and some Zambian citizens are involved in this," he said. Of course the government denied the allegation.

I flew to Zambia with my cameraman and quietly headed for Northwestern Province, under the pretext of reporting on the refugee situation at Maheba Camp in Mwinilunga. We asked a lot of question and found ourselves in a remote village outside Kasempa, on the border with Angola. Villagers told us about certain activities and we wanted this information on camera. Our driver did the interpretation. To our surprise a four-wheeled drive vehicle showed up from nowhere. Who could possibly come to such a remote place with a big vehicle? They were officials from the Zambian security forces. They told us that it was not safe for us to be in that area and we had to leave immediately. I refused to leave. I had a few bits of a juicy news story. I was warned that I'd be arrested. Being locked up for doing my job was not strange, but for some reason, I felt uncomfortable about being arrested in my own country. So we packed our gear and started the almost 600 kilometre disappointing drive back to Lusaka. It was late afternoon when we left and we got to Lusaka in the early hours of the morning. Authorities in Lusaka wouldn't speak to me. I even tried to solicit 'off record' information from my cousin at army headquarters who seemed to know something, but he wouldn't tell me anything.

I reported on the DRC peace talks in Zambia. The belligerent parties met in the country to iron out a peace deal to the long-drawn-out conflict. I had reliable sources, be they rebel groups, Zimbabwean, DRC, Namibian, Rwandan or Ugandan foreign ministries, fellow journalists and others. They provided first class information for my reporting. I also had good access to President Chiluba, who was chairing the talks. I sensed that my employers at the SABC were not too pleased with some of my reporting which appeared inclined towards Zambia's foreign policy on the DRC conflict. They later stopped me from reporting altogether and confined me to studio presenting.

During one of my interviews with President Chiluba, he pulled out a brown envelope and filled it with cash from his drawer. After the interview, he handed me the envelope saying it was for my mother. I was startled and refused to take it. He insisted I should. It was not uncommon for people to patronize State House for money directly from the presidency. It was drawn from what was known as 'the presidential slush fund'.

Small scale entrepreneurs and traders would frequent the place for help. I was surprised to learn that my mother had been there too. I could not argue against the president. I took the envelope. I'd left my handbag in the boot of the car parked outside State House when I went in for the interview so walking out of the executive office with a big brown envelope was a huge embarrassment. Dozens of people were in the lobby. I did the 500 metre walk of shame to the car park outside the gate. Those who saw me must have thought I'd gone to State House to ask for money. Even worse I felt those who knew me would be appalled by my lack of ethics and integrity. Journalists are not supposed to get money from politicians. Period! The sad part of it was that I couldn't explain to anyone that the money was for my mother. It wasn't possible. I gave my mother the envelope the same day and begged her never to go to State House again.

Political Aspirations

Despite my robust and exciting international diplomatic career, I made several attempts to work for my country, in a government position.

While at the SABC, I contacted a senior official at the Zambian High Commission in Pretoria to offer my services as press attaché. He said he'd look into it. Weeks later when I was in Lusaka, the official called a meeting with others from the Ministry of Foreign Affairs and State House who were very close to the president, to discuss my proposal. They were excited about my offer to serve my country and told me, "Consider it done." I never heard from them again and they didn't respond to my calls.

Well informed sources told me that a story had been cooked up about me that I was too close to foreign powers so I would not be expected to be loyal to my country. The source said they had seen a bad report about me in a file somewhere. I was also informed that in that file were fabricated letters purportedly written by me, denouncing my country. The person who wrote these letters is a former female colleague at ZNBC known to me.

I did not give up my aspiration to work for my country. After Chiluba left office, I approached the administration of President Mwanawasa to discuss the same. Again high profile people were involved in this 'recruitment' process. I offered to serve in any capacity they saw fit, but was keen on international relations. They asked for my CV. On February 26, 2002 while still working for the BBC, I got a heads-up via phone that President Mwanawasa would be in London on the 28th and that I should meet him at a certain hotel for a radio interview. I had interviewed him earlier, before he went to the US. In our discussion, he asked me if I thought he was 'a cabbage', as others had teased him. I said certainly not, with a giggle. Now on his return, I was also to meet the others after the planned second interview to finalise the job issue.

I showed up at the hotel an hour early. I was happy to meet the Zambian delegation. It was always a pleasure to see people from home and to catch up on the latest news. After waiting for two hours, I and other journalists on the presidential delegation were shown to the briefing room where we set up our recording equipment. Then I heard the door to a nearby room open. I took a quick glance and saw that the presidential spokesperson had been summoned.

The gentleman walked back into the room where we were with a sullen face. He told us that the interview was off. He didn't say why. Baffled, I insisted on knowing. There was no explanation. Then I asked to meet with the other officials to discuss my job request. I was told they were not available either. Disappointed, I packed my equipment, walked to the nearby underground station and took the train to the office.

My follow-up calls to the people I was to have met, after they returned to Zambia, went unanswered. I wondered what happened to the promised interview and the meeting. How could people who were so eager to meet me that they even called from the US, suddenly not be available? I never found out why.

In 2010, two years after I joined the United Nations, an opportunity again presented itself for me to work for my country. Mr Rupiah Banda was president and the state was looking for a director general for the public broadcaster ZNBC, where I began my career more than twenty years earlier. What an honour and a dream come true it would be to go back in the most senior role, from where I started as a junior teenage journalist!

I believed that if these issues were discussed at a high level, such as with the head of state, they would be sorted out more quickly. At least that's what I was told. Besides, why go to the lower ranks when I had access to high office? I had met, interviewed, even wined and dined with many heads of state, so I was accustomed to mingling with powerful people. I felt even freer with my own presidents.

It was May, 2010. President Banda and veteran politician and diplomat Mr Vernon Mwaanga were in South Africa for the official opening of the FIFA World Cup. Mr Mwaanga was a regular visitor to Johannesburg for medical check-ups. Sometimes when he and his wife Edna were in town, we would meet up for dinner or lunch. It was at these meetings that I told him repeatedly that I wanted to go back home, but needed something substantive to go back to. It was agreed that I be considered for the ZNBC director general job. Over the months, I had worked on a turn-around strategy for the station and was eager to implement it. Mr Mwaanga and I go back a long way. He worked with my father at the Times of Zambia in the 1970s when I was a toddler. He was the editor-in-chief and my dad news editor. He was also the patron of the Leopards Hill Secondary School, where I was a pioneer student and one of the top achievers. He has followed my career development over the years and offered guidance where possible. So I was happy and at ease to discuss my ambition.

I met with President Banda and Mr Mwaanga in Pretoria. We discussed the ZNBC job at length. The president's concern was how the organisation was going to remunerate me, factoring in my well-paying job at the UN. "We cannot match the UN package, so are you willing to take a drop in income?" President Banda asked.

I suggested that the Zambian government approach the UN for support. I told them of a similar case in Cambodia where the UN supported the secondment of the managing director post for Phnom Phen TV. A Cambodian media expert working for the UN was seconded to the TV station for three years. I was sure the same would work in my case. I was elated at the prospect of soon going where I'd begun. But the issue died a natural death!

The following year in September, 2011 the government in Zambia changed. Before then, I had diverted my rejection and frustration to quietly working with the opposition Patriotic Front (PF) in media and image campaigns. I would meet regularly with senior party officials, and an editor of a prominent newspaper, some of whom visited my home in Johannesburg to discuss media strategies well into the night. I drafted a comprehensive elections campaign communications plan which I promised to help implement. Hardly a day went by without my speaking to key members of the opposition on strategy. I even helped fly in a few international journalists to boost the public image of the opposition. I also flew to Lusaka regularly and was repeatedly promised a senior position if the opposition won the election. I used my international media contacts to influence positive reporting and image building of Mr Sata and the PF. I believed that this international perception would add impetus to the campaign back home. It actually worked.

Some in the PF suggested that I run as member of parliament for a constituency in Serenje, my home town, where I was almost assured of victory. I spoke to Chieftainess Serenje, a close relative and she said she'd mobilise other chiefs and the masses to give me the biggest landslide any parliamentary constituency in the country had ever seen. But I was not ready. It was July, only two months before the elections. I had not done any campaigning. I didn't have the resources either and spiritually, didn't feel ready. Besides, the PF secretariat had someone else in mind for that constituency, so I didn't want to waste my time. I preferred to work in the background.

The momentum for change in Zambia was growing. And we were certain that change would come. As expected, the PF won. I was now sure I would go back home. To my horror, the communication line with my acquaintances went quiet soon after Mr Sata was sworn in. None of them answered or returned my calls. I thought they were busy and needed time and space. They would get in touch with me after the dust had settled. They didn't.

I flew to Lusaka in the belief that being on the ground would move things. I was still employed by the United Nations but eager to get a political appointment. A senior official from the PF secretariat with whom I'd worked closely during the campaigns promised he'd pass on a word to the president about me. I never heard from him again. My other regular contact asked me to email my CV so that she could personally hand it over to the president because he was making the appointments. I never heard back from her either. She neither answered nor returned my calls.

I decided to see the president myself. After all, he was my "uncle". His wife was the Matron of Honour at my wedding. Getting an appointment was not too difficult. The president's principal secretary suggested I be there at 8 a.m. before it got too crowded. Every day hordes of people converged at State House wanting to speak to the president about jobs. He was the chief appointing officer.

Two other people were summoned into the same meeting with the President. I had hoped for privacy. They too had come to ask for jobs.

"Ms Nkandu, what can I do for you?" the president asked. I was seated far from his desk so he asked me to move closer. I told him that I had come to see him to discuss a role in government.

"What qualifications do you have?" he asked. I wondered whether he was pretending not to know me because there were others in the room or whether he was playing the true role of an HR manager.

"I have a Master's degree and many years' experience..." Before I finished my sentence, President Sata told me that he had better qualified people than me. "I have people with Doctorates so why should I give you a job?" he asked. I told him that I, too, had started studying part time for my Doctorate, though I'd stopped due to pressure of work. He wasn't paying attention and seemed disinterested in what I was saying.

I realised that I was in a serious job interview and had to market myself well. I took out a folder with my CV and motivational letter and handed it over to him. He briskly flipped through it then asked me where I was working.

"I am now with the UN your Excellency," I responded. President Sata then turned to his press aide who had been listening with a gleeful smile and asked him why Zambians from the UN were now asking him for jobs.

George Chellah chuckled and mumbled something inaudible, though it sounded as if he said, "because they love their country."

"The other day I had someone from the UN. Now you ... the UN office here in Lusaka still hasn't given me the special calendar I requested from them," the president said.

I didn't understand what the calendar had to do with it, but I apologised on behalf of the UN office and promised to follow it up. I tried to divert the discussion back to my job request but he dismissed me. He threw my papers into the 'pending' tray and told me that they would be in touch.

I had never felt so belittled in my life. I walked out of the president's office regretting having gone there in the first place. The other two who had come looking for a posting and sat in during my brisk interview session told me not to worry. They said that was President Sata's style. They assured me that he would get back to me. I never heard from him or from anyone in his government again. I decided to let it go.

When I told my dad what had happened, he scolded me. "I told you years ago never to get involved in politics in this country." He asked me why I would want to reduce myself to a "brush with the coal and cinder" when I was doing well on the international radar. He also said that if I had the burning desire to serve my country, I should let them come looking for me. This time, I took heed and decided to focus on my international career in the United Nations.

Losing Daddy

There was a cool breeze with gentle morning showers when my mobile phone rang at 4:55 a.m. It was my elder brother Dick calling to inform me that my father had passed away. His message was a very brief, "Sorry to inform you that our father has died." He waited for my reaction, then hung up. I could tell from the tone of his voice that he was very emotional. At eighty two, my dad died peacefully in his sleep.

Although he had been poorly for some time, news of his death disoriented me. I jumped out of bed, sat up and said a prayer. I mumbled a few incoherent words to God but am sure He heard my prayer because I asked for strength. I woke up my family in the house to tell them of the sad news. They all hugged me in comfort, knowing how close I was to Dad.

My father's passing came at a time when I had no money. I decided to fly to Lusaka the same day to take charge of funeral arrangements. This was my promise to him – that I'd make sure he was buried within three days and I'd ensure that there was no pomp and circumstance at his funeral. He was a simple, modest man who wanted a modest burial.

My family was amazed at how courageous I was. Being 'Daddy's girl' they had expected me to be in emotional tatters. Instead I was composed and tough. I was very close to my father, perhaps the closest. I was his favourite child. This earned me life-long resentment from my siblings. Hardly a week went by without me speaking to him. My life was intricately tied to his. I'd call him for advice, or to share news about an achievement at work, and to discuss my challenges.

When he grew older and had impaired speech following a mild stroke, it became hard to communicate with him. He, too, was frustrated. My father was an eloquent and articulate speaker, who'd mastered the English language well. He spoke the 'Queen's English'. He was a good scribe, perhaps the best-known journalist in Zambia. There are few in the profession who had not gone through his hand, in the form of communications and journalism training. He was also a prolific writer. I remember him editing the letters I sent to him when I was a student at university. He'd proofread then post the letters back to me with edits.

As far as my chosen profession was concerned, I ate 'straight from the pot'. I was taught by my dad. Every moment I spent with him was a lesson in media law, ethics, integrity, history, news and current affairs, politics, tradition and many other aspects of life. He instilled in me good values such as how being well dressed always made one confident. He taught me to be polished, all the time. In dress and in everything I did. I learned from him and my mother about etiquette and good manners. My dad taught me photography and film-making when I was nine years old. He also showed me how to write a newspaper article on his typewriter and even how to use one. And he instilled in me strong aspects of information gathering and security. He even taught me how to shoot with his .38 calibre pistol. He took my young brother and me to the bush and taught us to shoot birds. After three months of target practice, I never missed a shot.

On the day of his passing, I arrived in Lusaka the same night. I had to get there to prove to myself that he was indeed gone. I thought his passing would earn me empathy from my siblings. It didn't. We agreed that he'd be put to rest within three days of his passing as was his wish. Months earlier, I'd written to a few family members suggesting that we should plan what we would do when Dad finally left us. I got no response. Now the tragedy was upon us and there was no plan in place.

Funeral arrangements were hectic. I got support from old friends in Lusaka, both moral and financial support. It was as if they knew I was cash-strapped. They'd come by to see me and quietly slip bank notes or an envelope in my hand. The funds were helpful.

There was a deadlock on the night before burial because we couldn't agree on the programme. My brother, a full-time Jehovah's Witness suggested a programme that would be entirely based on his religious belief. He insisted that Dad was one and we had to follow that way. I wanted it partly secular. I know that my dad was not a committed Witness, but even if he was, it would have been good to incorporate both. By midnight, we'd still not agreed on who was going to speak. I rejected some names which my brother suggested, and he rejected the ones I proposed. We decided to leave the matter for the morning.

In the morning, my brother was nowhere to be seen and his phone was off. People were asking about the programme. We didn't have any. I had to think and act fast. Other family members also pulled out because they didn't agree with my plan. I thought it cruel. I realised I was alone and I had to get everything done quickly. We could not postpone to the following day. Burial space at the cemetery had already been secured and dug. Traditionally, it is taboo for a grave to lie open overnight. It's considered a bad omen, so postponing the burial was out of the question.

In the meantime, an old friend, Cosmas Chileshe, had been with me from the day my father died. He drove me around and helped to arrange things. We were introduced by my dad eighteen years earlier. Cosmas was Dad's former student. Cosmas was God-sent. He and I joined forces. We went to the funeral parlour to ensure that the body had been taken care of and all was in place. We got stuck in traffic and hit a few hitches along the way. Meanwhile, Cosmas, who worked for ZNBC, arranged for the announcement on the burial place and time. The two of us also sent out text messages to inform people. I decided mourners should go straight to the cemetery for body viewing and burial. There was no church to go to because, due to our disagreement, my brother had cancelled the service.

Viewing the dead is forbidden by the Watch Tower Society and it was the main bone of contention in the family. I saw the need to do it because people wanting to pay their last respects would have liked to see him. It didn't matter now. Dick and others had withdrawn from the programme and I had to deal with it. When I finally got hold of him later in the morning, he told me that for the sake of peace, they'd decided to pull out so that I do as I pleased. He and others would have nothing to do with the proceedings of the day.

While at the funeral parlour, I asked to use the manager's laptop and printer for the programme. He kindly agreed. Cosmas and I phoned people to ask if they would give tributes. Luckily all of them agreed.

As we approached midday all was set and we started off for the cemetery – the hearse carrying my father in front, Cosmas and I driving closely behind. I felt like breaking down but I couldn't - I had to be strong. Everything was in my hands now. People at the cemetery were getting impatient. Our phones rang every minute, from people asking what time we'd get there.

I could see the looks of shock and amazement when the hearse drove in, with only my friend and me accompanying it. I heard whispers: "What's going on?" "Why is she alone?" "She's very brave to drive down all alone with her father's body." I also overheard someone say that I was a bully and too stubborn for my own good. I ignored them all. I just wanted the process done, and done properly. The Jehovah's Witness group did not attend body viewing. We handed out the programme as people filed past my father's coffin.

All the people who'd committed to speak showed up and gave profound statements, except for the pastor, whom we'd asked to offer prayers. He didn't pitch up. I could feel the blood in me flush on my face. By now I was sure my siblings were waiting to see me fail. This was not new. They had done this to me several times before. Cosmas stepped in and prayed, amid wails of protest from family members who felt the prayer should have been by an elder from the Kingdom Hall. Cosmas ignored them. When my father's body was interred, I had a sense of relief instead of the normal grief that would engulf one when their loved one was being buried.

It occurred to me that Dad had repeatedly asked me to be strong because he knew what lay ahead. The last time I saw him before he passed away, I nearly broke down as I was leaving. Struggling to speak, he said, "My daughter, you are a man and real men don't cry."

I was the last to pay tribute to him at the graveside. But in the end, I couldn't hold back. It all came crashing on me. I broke down helplessly. My relationship with him in life and in death was the same - one which brought on division and resentment from my siblings and other relatives. Like always, I didn't care! And that is how we buried Dad.

As people dispersed, having hugged each other and given words of comfort, I gripped Cosmas' hand tight. He and I walked steadily to his car, oblivious of everything and everyone around us. We sat in the vehicle and looked at each other, and we both said, "It's over; we've done it."

The days that followed were hollow and painful. It was only then that I realised my dad was gone forever. I suppose it was God's way to make me very busy and frantic as a coping mechanism.

Although he died a peaceful death, I know that my father also died a sad man. He was displeased at the state of politics and the media. As a former freedom fighter, it was painful to see that half a century on, most

Zambians still lived in poverty. He decried the poor standard of education, social and moral decay. Often when we chatted, he'd throw scorn on the calibre of leaders in parliament and in government. "Some of them belong to the gutters," he said.

My father gave up an international career to serve his country. He was passionate about media development and spent most of his late adult years lecturing, mentoring and trying to uplift the standards of journalists. We spoke regularly about media and politics not only in Zambia, but also in the rest of the continent. His assertion was that they were interlinked. Lack of adequate investment in the media by both the private and public sectors killed the profession. Journalist were undertrained, poorly paid and lived in deplorable conditions. This made them vulnerable and easy prey to politicians whom he said turned even the best of scribes into propaganda and cheap political mouth-pieces. "You cannot entirely blame journalists. Newsrooms these days are run by journalists who sell out because they fear for their jobs and livelihood. So they have thrown away all their good training simply to survive.... In my days as a news editor, I could tell a politician to go to hell and slam the phone on him. Maybe that's why I never got a political appointment," said my dad, with a naughty smile on his face.

He bemoaned the lack of creativity, ethics and understanding of the role of media in national growth and security. "Instead of using media for propaganda, a partnership for development could be established, so that focus is on promoting the development agenda and filtering key messages to all sectors of society on citizens' participation."

In a wide-ranging interview I had with him after the August 2016 elections, my dad also said that the average Zambian did not understand the link between their level of poverty and political process. "This explains why they attend rallies, drink and dance then vote for a politician or party based on the containers of *Shake-Shake* or *chitenge* material they are given at election rallies. Campaigns are not issue-based," he said. I asked him if he ever regretted having put in so much for his country only to be side-lined by successive administrations. "No, not at all," said my father.

"Everything I did had to be done."

In Conclusion

Losing my dad just before I turned fifty was a turning point for me. It symbolised the start of a new life - the metamorphosis from 'Daddy's girl' to a middle-aged Maureen. A few months after he departed, I was terrified. There were a lot of changes in my life - physical and emotional, brought on by stress and the pain of losing him; as well as a change in my professional outlook. I'd often turn to him for advice, guidance or just to share news about myself, and my children. I felt secure with him around. I had a recurring dream when I was growing up; I'd dream that thieves were trying to break into the house or had got in and were about to attack me and my family. I'd run to knock on my parents' room door and my dad would come out with his gun to protect us. I had the dream all the time, for years. It stopped after my dad passed away.

But now I needed a change. A part of me wanted to go back to journalism, my passion, to honour my father's wish. He'd wanted me to go back to TV. He said that's where I was born and that's where I belonged.

I felt that the passing of my dad symbolised a new season. So, what was I to do? I was employed at eighteen, had a child just before I turned twenty one and had been married and travelled to half the world by the time I hit thirty. When I was forty I said that being president of Zambia or UN secretary general was my goal. I'd walked the corridors of power, wined and dined with the mink and manure, shared stories of the impoverished, downtrodden and war stricken to the world and worked in the world's best organisations. I felt that my next move had to be either very small or massive.

I got a good job offer from an international news network based in Nairobi, but sadly had to turn it down because it didn't tie in well with my domestic situation. Perhaps the most difficult challenge I faced was juggling a highly demanding career with being a good mother and a wife. The husband fell by the wayside so I became a single mother years ago, and excelled. I'd imagine that for any young woman wanting to be a successful journalist, getting married or having children, would be grossly difficult to balance. It is the most difficult thing I have ever done, but I have achieved good results: an educated and married daughter, an intelligent and politically astute son at university, and a younger son with an IQ of 122; that's my success story!

People ask me about how I've managed my career and my domestic life and how I've had a steady upward trajectory. But what is success? I always quote the late Nelson Mandela who said, "Success is not what I have done and achieved, but how many times I got up, after I fell." For me, being successful involves hard work and a lot of sacrifices. It's been my upbringing to exceed expectations through discipline and determination, so it comes naturally in my career life. I do what I like, what I think is right and what impacts positively on others. My work ethic has done me good. I stay focused on being professional. My secret is to enjoy what I do, because if it is interesting, rewarding, challenging and making me a better person then I'll do it well. I walk away immediately I lose the passion.

I have also learned a lot about the resilience of the human spirit. How people strive to excel or achieve high goals in whatever they do, as well as how those in very difficult circumstances hold on to life and get by. The most important lesson of all, Carpe Diem *(Seize the Day)* and be happy.

As I begin my next half century journey, I ask myself what my goal or ambition is. A few years ago, I'd have consulted my father. But I've come to realise that not all his influence on me was positive, his political stance for instance: he resented Zambian politics and urged me not to get involved. He said I'd mess up my life if I joined politics. I felt otherwise. I believed that I had a lot to contribute. I respected his principles which he took with him to his grave. When my father died, he had only few possessions. Among them his old typewriter, a pen and note book. He said he'd die with these. They were worth more than any other material wealth. I have now inherited them. I know that despite my father being angry, bitter and resentful of a system that let him down, he died a proud man, for he stuck to what he believed in. I promised him that I would emulate his ways, for it was the right thing to do.

Transforming lives for the better is my ultimate goal. I still have a special place for my country, despite all my past pain and sorrow. I visit Zambia frequently, especially because the reasons why I left no longer exist. At 50, my life has turned-full circle and I know that I will return one day, as a servant-leader.

Printed in the United States
By Bookmasters